ALL MOROCCO

Photographs: Fotolia.com and Photographic Archives of FISA-Escudo de Oro.

Text, design, lay-out and printing entirely
created by the technical department of
EDITORIAL FISA ESCUDO DE ORO, S.A.

Distributor in Morocco:
Société Marocaine d'Etude d'Edition
et de Promotion SMEEP sarl
Résidence Select Magasin numero 13 Place Mauritanie
Ville Nouvelle Meknes Morocco
Tel: 06 24 25 33 38
med.matioui@gmail.com

ESCUDO DE ORO

Beach near Tangier.

Situated at the western end of North Africa, also known as Africa Minor, Berbery, or Maghreb, the Kingdom of Morocco has a coastline that stretches from the Mediterranean to the Atlantic: a natural frontier. The Mediterranean coast is rugged, but the Atlantic side is much less so and has many fine beaches. A large fertile plain abounding in valleys and hills stretches between the Atlantic and the mountains.

The Draa Valley.

The Atlas Mountains –the peak at Toubkal reaches a height of 4,165 metres– are the spinal column of western Morocco, and the Rif mountains encircle the Mediterranean area.

Man's presence in this country dates from prehistoric times, as is shown by the discovery of fossilized human skeletons near Rabat, Casablanca and other cities, dating from the earlier and mid-paleolithic age and belonging to a human race with the same characteristics as Neanderthal man. It would appear that Morocco was inhabited during the later Palaeolithic age by a race very similar to homo sapiens. During the Neolithic age Phoenicians and Carthaginians reached northern Africa and Morocco entered history as a country. After the arrival of the Berbers, Morocco was occupied by the Romans, Vandals and Byzantines. But the real history of Morocco began with the Arab conquest and the establishment of Islam at the end of the 3th century by Sherif Moulay Idris, great-grandson of Ali, son-in-law of Mohammed. It was Idris II, the posthumous son of Moulay Idris, who founded the first kingdom of Morocco.

Berber village in the Atlas Mountains.

Caravan in the Erg Chebbi Dunes, near Merzouga.

The Triumphal Arch of Emperor Caracalla in Volubilis.

Later on the Berber kingdoms of Berghouata, in what is now Chaouia, and Sijilmassa in the region of the oases, and the Arab kingdom of the Idrisids were created. When Idris II died at the beginning of the 9th century Berber kingdoms were again established in Morocco.

There was later a second Arab invasion, and in the 10th century the Almoravids founded a great empire in what is now Morocco. In the 12th century, the Almohad Ibn Toumert founded a new dynasty. His successor, Abd al Mumin, conquered the Moroccan Atlas and the main cities of Algeria, Tunisia and Andalusia. His son and grandson expanded the empire further, but the whole Almohad Empire fell in the 13th century. Then came the Marinids and the Saadis, whose respective dynasties helped to establish Morocco's artistic and cultural heritage.

In the middle of the 17th century, the Alawis replaced the Saadis and founded a dynasty,

Meknes: Mausoleum of Moulay Ismail.

established by Moulay Ismail in Meknes, which had the honour of founding modern Morocco. Its independence was recognized by Mohammed V, rejecting the protectorates imposed by France and Spain. His son, His Majesty Hassan II, when he reintegrated the territory of the Sahara to his kingdom in 1975, consolidated the independence of the country.

At present, Morocco boasts nine sites inscribed on the UNESCO World Heritage list: the medinas (old towns) of Fez, Marrakesh, Rabat, Meknes, Tetouan, Essaouira and El Jadida; Ksar of Ait-Ben-Haddou, near Ouarzazate, and the Archaeological Site of Volubilis.

The traditional fantasia or "gunpowder race".

Traditional dresses.

Morocco's skilled craftsmen produce fine leather goods, pottery, wickerwork, marquetry and kilims.

GASTRONOMY

Moroccan cuisine, thanks to its wise use of ingredients and methods of cooking, is rightly considered one of the most refined in the world. These are traditions, too, which go back over a thousand years, the fruit of recipes passed down, in the main, from mother to daughter.

Brkoukss (Couscous Soussi).

The principal ingredients in the cuisine of Morocco are provided by the rich fruits of the land and by lamb, beef or veal and chicken, as well as fish. This is, then, complete, nutritional fare. The best-known traditional Moroccan dishes are tagine, couscous, b'stilla (pie) and kebabs. Tagine is, in reality,

Pastilla and lamb tagine.

the name of the earthenware pot or bowl with the cone-shaped top (tagine) in which this meat and vegetable stew, usually based on lamb, is made. B'stilla, on the other hand, is a much more sophisticated dish, both in terms of number of ingredients and the preparation process. Couscous is another delicacy that takes its name from the recipient in which it is made, and which consists of a lower pan in which vegetables and meat are cooked, and a perforated upper pan in which ta'am, semolina made from flour, is steam cooked. Lamb, beef or kefta (mince) kebabs are always grilled over a charcoal fire.
The only drink at meal times is water. Mint tea, practically the national drink, is taken throughout the day. It is served in small glasses, its aromas best appreciated if it is slowly sipped. Mint tea is made according to a strict ritual. According to taste, aromatic herbs such as wormwood or orange flower may be added.

Shish kebabs.

Tea ready to serve.

Overall view of Rabat.

The Royal Guard.

Capital of the Kingdom of Morocco and seat of its government, Rabat is situated at the mouth of the river Bu Regreg, opposite the city of Sale. From the Hassan tower, dominating the ruins of the old mosque of which it was the minaret, there is a fine panoramic view with Rabat in the foreground, the estuary of the Bu Regreg, Salé, Chellah –the Roman *Sala Colonia*– and, on the horizon, the leafy wood of Mamora. Rabat consists of two clearly delineated areas: the medina, picturesque and full of vitality, and the new city with its modern urban development.

Rabat is a very old city and was among the resorts of Tingitania. The historian Ptolemy named it Sale. Apparently it acquired the status of a Roman municipality in the time of Trajan. Its present name, however, dates from the 8th century when Salih, the Berber chief of the Berghouta tribe, became a heresiarch of Islam and to defend himself from the orthodox built a *ribat*, which is a sort of fortified monastery. Towards the

Medina of Rabat.

middle of the 12th century, the Almohads attacked the Berghouata, and a century later the Marinids replaced the Almohads.
Rabat was the place of many brilliant historical events during numerous centuries; and after being the seat of the Residency General during the French Protectorate, it became the administrative capital of the kingdom when independence was granted to Morocco under Mohammed V. At the present time Rabat has the attractive appearance of a warm, welcoming city, rationally urbanized. Although it is the administrative capital of Morocco, it still preserves the charm of a former provincial capital. The typically Moroccan buildings are characterized by the elegant style that the sovereigns of the reigning dynasty have lent to their architecture.
Rabat is a city full of trees and flowers, with delightful gardens in agreeable contrast with the city buildings. A walk through the Belvedere Garden, the Oudaïa Garden, the Triangle Garden or the Experimental Garden is a real pleasure.
The most outstanding streets in Rabat are the Avenue Mohammed V, the busiest in

The Royal Palace.

the entire city, the Boulevard Hassan II, Rue Souq es Sebat, Place Souq el Ghezel and Rue Jamaa, the largest street in the attractive Kasbah of the Oudaïa dynasty. The whole city is filled with surprises for the tourist's eye.
Besides the Hassan Tower –the minaret of a Roman/ Byzantine style mosque considered to be one of the greatest temples of Islam–, whose elegant silhouette reminds one of the Koutoubia in Marrakesh and the Giralda in Seville, the following monuments are of prime importance both historically and artistically: the Royal Palace,

The Chellah Garden.

The Chellah Gate.

Ruins of the Chellah and its mosque.

Walls of the Udayas fortress. KASBAH

The Udayas Garden.

Bab Alruah, or the Gate of the Winds, in the Almohad walls.

Esplanade and Hassan Tower.

Hassan Tower.

the Chellah, the city walls, the gateway of the Kasbah of the Oudaïa dynasty, the Bâb Er Rouah gate, the 14th-century Marinid fountain, the Great Mosque, the small Guazzarin Mosque and Mohammed V's mausoleum.

The Royal Palace was built during the second half of the 19th century on a site formerly occupied by the Palace of Sidi Mohammed ben Abdallah. Its most impressive feature is the majestic gateway in yellow stone. The large, sumptuous chambers have been restored

Fountain in the Mausoleum of Mohammed V.

Mausoleum of Mohammed V.

Tomb of Mohammed V. ▶

and extensively decorated in recent years.
The Chellah is situated at the entrance to Rabat. This is a former Roman city of great architectural value, considered to be «the most romantic spot in Morocco».
Mohammed V's mausoleum is located on the esplanade of the Hassan mosque. The monarch's tomb is in a vast room with artistically decorated marble walls with a fine cedar-wood dome encrusted with gold leaf.
There are several extremely interesting museums in Rabat. In the Archaeological Museum there are works of incalculable value, the most outstanding of which are objects from the principal archaeological sites in the country, the geometrical mosaic from Volubilis that sums up the ancient history of Morocco, a large royal statue in white marble, jewels, cameos, and other interesting pieces.
The Museum of Moroccan Arts, the Scientific Institute and the Museum of Earth Sciences all have noteworthy collections.
There are many beaches in the environs of Rabat, among them those known as Little Smugglers, Temara, Golden Valley, Krick Rock, Golden Sands, Skhirat and Oued Ykem.
Another big tourist attraction of the Moroccan capital is its proximity to **Salé**, Rabat's twin city, surrounded by an exceptionally beautiful landscape and featuring many interesting monuments.

Together with Fez, Marrakesh and Rabat, Meknes makes up the quartet of Morocco's imperial cities. It is surrounded by a triple protective wall with bastions and is made up of two clearly distinguishable areas, the modern and the old parts. In the Medina there are still several monuments dating from before the Alawite dynasty, but the present-day city grew up with the architectural style of Moulay Ismail, who reigned in the 18th century.

The name of the city is derived from that of the Meknassa, the great Berber tribe that founded Taza and Meknes. After the rule of the Almoravids, the Almohads reigned, and then the Marinids. Abu Yusuf Ya'qub al-Mansur built a new Kasbah and an enormous mosque in the second half of the 13th century, then Abu el Hassan and his son Abu Inan consolidated Meknes' urban design. After a series of vicissitudes the Alawid Sultan Moulay Ismail ennobled the city by building numerous monuments, and established close ties with the France of Louis XIV. On the death of this glorious Alawid sovereign, the city went into decline for a short time, but Sultan Sidi Mohammed Ben Abdallah was still able to provide Meknes with several mosques and to build the mausoleums of Sidi Mohammed Ben Alssa and Sidi Bou Othman. In 1755 the imperial city was affected by the earthquake that destroyed Lisbon. In 1908, Meknes played an active part in the dethrone-

Overall view of Meknes.

ment of Sultan Moulay Abd al-Aziz. He was replaced by Moulay Afiz, in turn dethroned three years later; this gave rise to the occupation of Meknes by the French, which continued until 1956.

The Medina is of particular interest, embracing Rue Rouamazin –full of bustle and colour–, Rue Dar Smen, Place El Kdim, Bâb Mansour el Aleuj, and Dar Jamai. The visitor should also see the former imperial city with the large Place Lalla Aouda, Dar Kebira,

View of Meknes from Bad el Berdaine.

Bab Mansour Gate.

Entrance to the Dar Jamai Museum, housed in a sumptuous palace and devoted to Moroccan art.

Bab el-Khemis Gate.

Moulay Ismail Gate.

the tomb of Moulay Ismail, the Garden of the Sultans, Dar el Makhzen, Bâb en Nouar and Bâb Merah; and the modern city with the Town Hall and the Law Courts. The markets and commercial galleries at Meknes are particularly attractive: it is possible to buy anything from magnificent Berber carpets to all kinds of artistic Moroccan craft work here.

The outstanding monuments here are the walls; the colossal Bab el Mansour gate –of majestic proportions, begun shortly before the death of Moulay Ismail and finished around 1732 by his son Moulay Abdallah–, the largest in Meknes and one of the most famous in the whole of North Africa; the palace of Dar Jamai, built towards the end of the 19th century, with the rooms around its beautiful garden converted since 1926 into the Museum of Moroccan Art; the artistic gate of Bab el Khémis; the astonishingly beautiful Bab Berdaïne gate built by Moulay Ismail; Moulay Ismail's granaries, consisting of a vast area divided into twenty-three sections; the Hara's prison or

Mausuleum of Moulay Ismail.

Christians' prison, where the European captives who worked on the fortifications lived in a vast underground space; and the fine mosques –especially Bab Berrima– appearing here and there with their characteristic architecture.

The gardens, surrounded by high walls, have a special charm in Meknes. The most outstanding are Djenan Es Souani, the Sultan's Garden and the Experimental Garden. Another outstanding attraction in the city is the Bou Inania Madrasa. Like its counterpart in Fez, it was built in the middle of the 14th century by the Merinites. Very well conserved, its exquisite decoration makes this a veritable jewel in the crown of Islamic art. The Madrasa is an ancient Quran school where, besides religion, pupils could also study other subjects, such as mathematics, medicine and other sciences.

Pleasant excursions may be undertaken from Meknes: to **Volubilis**, 31 kilometres away, where the most important Roman ruins in Morocco stand; to **Moulay Idriss**, the holy city where the most important *moussem* in Morocco takes place, to which thousands of pilgrims flock; or to the luxuriant **oases** that lie ten kilometres to the west of Meknes.

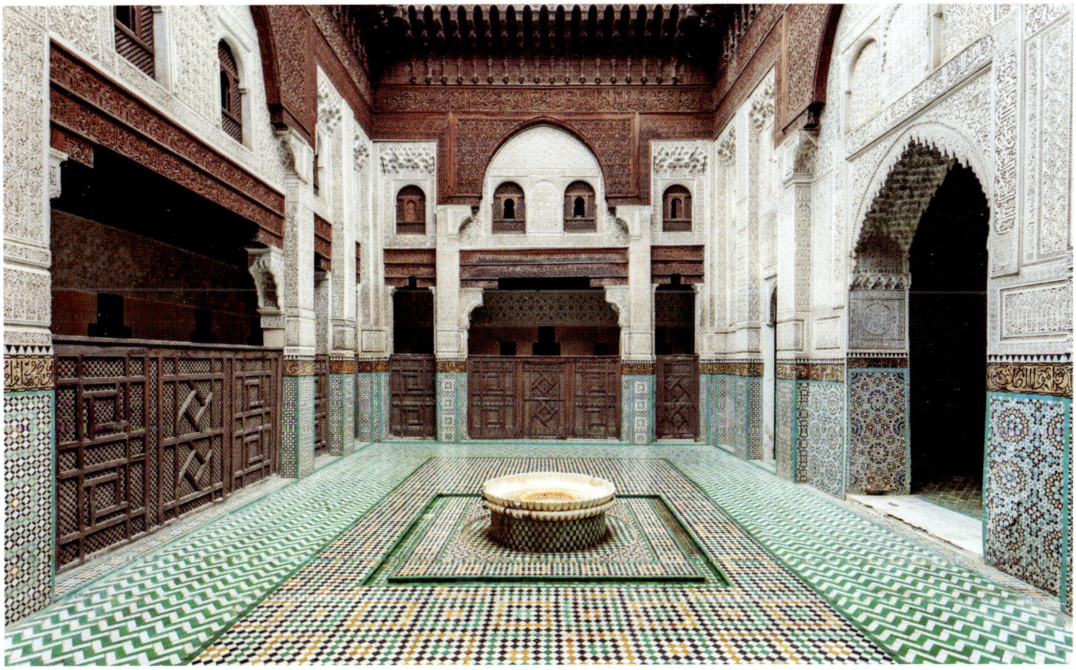

Madrasa Bou Inania.

Volubilis: mosaics.

Volubilis: House of Columns.

Volubilis: House of Bacchus.

Volubilis: House of Orpheus.

The Holy City of Moulay Idriss.

Fez is the oldest of Morocco's imperial cities. Founded in 808 by Idris II, it quickly became an important trading centre and after three centuries under the Marinid dynasty it was a great city whose artistic and intellectual prestige had become known even in Europe. Fez conserves to this day the attractive appearance of a mediaeval Islamic city. The Marinid kings and those of the Alawid dynasty embellished the city with numerous monuments, many of them still excellently preserved, constituting good examples of the Hispano-Moorish style.

The old city –Fez el Bali, founded by Idris II– is joined to the new one, Fez el-Jdid, by the lovely gardens of Boujeloud, near Dar el Batha Museum and

Overall view of Fez.

the palace of Dar el Beida. The city of Fez is so extraordinarily beautiful that an Arab historian was heard to say: «Oh Fez! All the beauties of the earth are to be found in thee!».

Though the foundation of Fez is attributed to Idris II, his father, Idris I, a descendant of the Prophet, was the first to settle here, in around the year 786 or 787. After its foundation Fez welcomed many Andalusian Moslems, who helped to develop what was to be the imperial capital of Morocco. Later, in the 11th century, the Almoravids estab-

Boujloud Gardens.

lished themselves in Fez, but not without having to overcome the bitter opposition of the Beni Hammad. The Almohads succeeded the Almoravids in the 12th century, and contributed to the magnificence of the city of Fez. In the early 13th century the Marinids succeeded in eliminating the Almohads, and during the reigns of Abou er Rabi and Abou Saïd Othman in the 14th century Fez achieved extraordinary prosperity. In the 15th century Mohammed ech Cheikh, son of Yahia, the Ouattasside governor murdered by order of the last Marinid sultan, Abd el Haqq, had himself proclaimed sovereign in Fez. The Ouattasside dynasty was substituted in the 16th century by that of the Saadis, and Fez lost its status as capital of the kingdom. The city suffered several changes of fortune, but in the 18th century –during the reign of Moulay Abdallah– it became the capital once more. The Alawid dynasty contributed considerably to the greatness of the imperial capital. In the

Dar Batha Museum.

The Royal Palace.

Fez: the New City.

Bab Boujloud Gate.

Bab Chorfa Gate.

19th century Moulay El Hassan made many changes in Fez, and it was during his reign that the Boujloud palace and other important monuments were built. Taking advantage of the internal rivalries undermining the Sultan's authority, the French occupied Fez in 1911, and in 1912 established a protectorate which lasted until 1956.
According to tradition, the origin of the city's name derives from the fact that, when digging to lay the foundations –«in a valley situated between two high mountains covered with rich forests and watered by a thousand streams, to the right of the river of Pearls»– a large sickle (in Arabic, fez) weighing sixty pounds was found, and gave its name to the new imperial city. Fez was called the Mecca of the West and the Athens of Africa; in the 11th century it had a population of more than half a million inhabitants including Moors, Berbers, Jews, Negroes, Turks, Christians and renegades (Christians converted to Islam).
The writer Edmondo d'Amicis said of Fez in 1876 that «The city stretches out in the shape of a vast figure of eight between two hills, on whose summits stand the ruins of two ancient square fortresses. Beyond the hills is a range of mountains. The river of Pearls divides the city into two: New Fez on the left

Bou Inania Madrasa: minaret and courtyard of ablutions.

Courtyard in the Attarine Medersa.

Courtyard in the Karaouine Mosque. ▶

bank and old Fez on the right; and old battlements with great dark towers, broken down in many parts, surround both the old and new areas. From the heights one can get a good view of the whole city: a myriad of white houses with flat roofs, with fine minarets made out of mosaic towering above, gigantic palms, masses of green, crenellated towers, and small green domes. At first glance one can imagine the greatness of the ancient metropolis». Fez still continues to be an impressive city for its splendid, enchanting and pure evocation of mediaeval times. There is an extraordinary wealth of monuments in this great imperial city, which still today is one of the most dynamic religious and political centres in Morocco. The outstanding sights are the medersas of Bou Inania (with its original minaret), es Seffarine, el Attarine, Es-Sahrij, and Misbahiya; the El Qaraouiyyîn mosque, where there are sixteen aisles and 270 columns; the Andalusian's mosque with its colossal doorway; and the *zaouiya* of Moulay Idris, where the remains of the founder of Fez lie buried. But in truth the whole city is a delightful, fascinating monument, especially the old part. Another well-known feature of Fez are the traditional tanneries, where vats full of natural dyes and an intense smell create a colourful landscape.

There are some interesting excursions to be taken from the imperial city, among them is one to visit the large tomb where the princes of the Marinid dynasty lie buried, from whence the magnificent outline of the old city can be seen. A little further from the city, 15 and 22 kilometres distant, respectively, are the spas of **Sidi Harazem** and **Moulay Yacoub**, considered the finest thermal springs in Morocco. Moreover, going southwards direction we can visit the cool mountain landscapes of **Ifrane** and **Azrou**.

Zaouia of Moulay Idriss II.

Nejjarine fountain.

Traditional tannery: a must-see in Fez.

View of the Medina of Fez from the Tombs of the Marinids.

Overall view of Casablanca.

The commercial and industrial capital of Morocco, Casablanca is most highly-populated city in the kingdom. Full of light and hospitality, Casablanca honours its name. Usually known simply as Casa (in Arabic Dar el Beida, «White House»), it stretches over a wide area; and its large port, situated between the promontories of Oukacha and El Hank sheltering it, has the best port installations in the whole of the African continent. No other city of Morocco can dispute with Casablanca its status as the economic capital. The growth of this city is comparatively recent, starting at the beginning of the 20th century. After World War II its industrial development increased very

Park of the Arab League.

rapidly; it is Morocco's foremost port and one of the busiest in all Africa: an important port of call between Europe, Africa and South America, especially Brazil and Argentina.
The greater part of Casablanca's urban outline has been carried out according to the plans drawn up by the French architects Prost and Ecochart. The city is nowadays in constant expansion, following the lines of systematic Moroccanization, which became in 1956, the year in which the country attained its independence.
The appearance of the city is distinguished architecturally by the presence of large, modern buildings, contrasting markedly with other, typically Arab, edifices. The centre of Casablanca is dominated by the attractive green of the magnificent Arab League Park, and its broad avenues have fine views that are comparable with those of any of the most famous thoroughfares in Paris or New York.

Fountain in Mohammed V Square.

Apparently, the area where Casablanca now stands was inhabited by man during the Palaeolithic era. The city's origins are not known with any degree of exactitude, but it would appear that the ancient city of *Anfa* was located on the same site as the present-day city. Anfa played an important part in the history of Morocco at the end of the 7th century and at the beginning of the 8th century, and enjoyed particular renown in the 12th and 13th centuries. The corsairs of Anfa

Mohammed V Square: the courts.

United Nations Square, and walls of the old Medina.

Old Medina: Dar el-Makhzen Mosque.

were attacked in 1468 by a powerful squadron commanded by Ferdinand of Portugal; and the city suffered a further attack by the Portuguese in 1515. Sixty years later the Portuguese settled in the old city, which was fortified and rebuilt and given the name Casa Blanca. Incessant attacks by neighbouring tribes and the destruction wrought by the terrible earthquake of 1755 obliged the Portuguese to leave Casablanca. In the reign of Sidi Mohammed ben Abdallah (1757-1790) it was populated by Berbers. The city was again fortified and reconstructed; at this time it was called Dar el Beida, from which the Spaniards derived the name Casablanca. In the 18th century the city became an important trading centre and about the middle of the 19th century this commercial role was augmented; in 1862 there was a regular service between Marseilles and Morocco. At the beginning of the 20th century work on the building of the modern port was undertaken, and this constituted the basis of Casablanca's present-day economic development.

The economic importance of the city has not hindered its constantly increasing attraction for the tourist, as with the proximity to fine beaches surrounded by luxuriant vegetation and the splendid hotels, it is an ideal centre. The beaches at Pont-Blondin, Sehb Edheb, Temara, Miramar, El Harhoura, Tamaris and Azemmour (fringed with eucalyptus trees) are attractive spots for the tourist. The city also has splendid

Entrance to the New Medina.

sports facilities for golf, tennis, riding, sailing and other activities, along with many establishments of the highest category.
It is a delight to explore the city and to walk through the enchantingly picturesque old Moslem quarters. Place Mohammed V is the busiest part of Casablanca and its most important avenues are Avenue de l'Armée Royale, Boulevard Mohammed al Hansali leading from Place Mohammed V to the harbour, and literally crammed with shops and boutiques, and Avenue Hassan II. Place des Nations Unies is another important centre. In the old medina, a picturesque labyrinth of small streets, a visit is recommended to the mosque Dar el-Majzen or Great Mosque, and to the Sidi el Kairouani sanctuary, built at the 18th century in honour of Sidi Allal el Kairouani, high dignitary of Casablanca. Also well worth a visit is the New Medina or Habous, neighbourhood. The architecture in this area, where construction began in 1923, evokes the old Medinas of Morocco. The most outstanding sites here include the Royal Palace, the Mahakma (which

The Royal Palace.

Mahakma of the Pasha.

More than half of the mosque stands amid the ocean waters.

The exterior fountains in the mosque are star-shaped.

once housed the courts) and the mosques of Moulay Youssef and Mohammed V.

THE HASSAN II MOSQUE

After the death of his royal highness King Mohammed V in 1961, his son Hassan II considered building a mausoleum for his father in Casablanca, where the sad event had taken place. However, the sovereign eventually decided against the idea and ordered its construction in Rabat, in order to always have his father's tomb close at hand. This decision also allows heads of states visiting the capital to meditate or pray before the tomb of Mohammed V should they wish to do so. Nevertheless, having reached this conclusion, Hassan II felt he was indebted to the inhabitants of Casablanca and pledged to redress this by building a great mosque there, close to the sea.

Today, those fortunate enough to see the result of this personal project of the Moroccan king are overwhelmed with admiration when contemplating the imposing profile of the finished building. Majestic and inspiring, the temple appears to rise out of the depths of the Atlantic ocean. Indeed, one of the principle attractions of the Mosque is that two thirds of it were constructed over water. This remarkable accomplishment being inspired by two verses of the Koran which state «The throne of God was upon the waters» and «From water have we created all life». Another fact which may give some idea of the singular

Hassan II Mosque: south façade.

Details on the south façade.

nature of the Hassan II Mosque is the fact that it is the tallest religious building in the world, and the second largest in area of the Muslim world, after the Al Haramayn Acharifain Mosque in Mecca.

While the expanse of the Hassan II Mosque is vast, its spiritual significance for the entire Arabic and Islamic world is even greater. Situated at the extreme north-west point of what Muslims call *Dar al Islam* (the land of Islam), the Mosque proffers itself as a meeting point for the diverse civilizations which surround Morocco: the African, European, Mediterranean and Arab cultures. Thus, the sanctuary stands like a beacon, to guide an Islamic culture steeped in history on its search for greater tolerance and understanding of and from its neighbours.

The great Hassan II Mosque covers a surface area of 9 hectares. 12,500 workers, of which 10,000 were craftsmen and the rest labourers, toiled day and night in shifts in order to complete the building. To get some idea of the sheer size of the building it would be instructive to look at some

Prayer Room.

One of the domes that adorn the Prayer Room roof.

King Hassan II himself took a significant role in the construction. As the true father of the project, he personally supervised the pace of building and brought to the project many ideas and suggestions. The team of Moroccan architects and engineers, directed by Michel Pinseau, came to count on the active and enthusiastic participation of his majesty, who never hesitated in visiting the site whenever it was necessary.

Of a rectangular ground plan, the Hassan II Mosque is remarkable for its size, its impressive 200 metres high minaret which carves out the sky as it towers over Casablanca and, above all, for the extreme care which

of the statistics involved in its construction. 300,000 cubic metres of cement were used and 40,000 tons of steel. 65,000 tons of marble and 40,000 square metres of ornamented cedar wood were utilized in its decoration. Fifty million man-hours were needed during the six years of its elaboration.

Ablution Room.

has been taken over every detail of the interior. In all, the temple remains the pearl of a religious and cultural complex which also includes a museum, a library, a medersa (Islamic University), rooms set aside for seminars and meetings, a subterranean four lane driveway and an underground car park with capacity for 1,100 cars and 40 coaches.

The Hassan II Mosque by night.

Walls of El Jadida.

El Jadida, the ancient *Mazagan*, is situated in a magnificent sandy bay with rocks at either end. The remains of the old fortifications are conserved as vestiges of two and half centuries of Portuguese occupation. El Jadida used to be an important port on Morocco's Atlantic coast. At present, its outstandingly mild climate and sheltered beach make it one of the most attractive tourist centres in the kingdom.
El Jadida apparently occupies the same site as a for-

Minaret on the main mosque in El Jadida.

mer Phoenician trading post known as *Rusibis*, mentioned by Polybius, Ptolemy and Pliny the Elder. The Portuguese settled here in 1502 and built a fortress called el Brijia El Jadida. The city itself was also founded by the Portuguese, in 1506, and given the name Mazagan; it later became the most important Portuguese trading post on the Atlantic coast. In 1562, the Saadi Moulay Abdallah attacked the fortress but was unable to capture it. From 1580 to 1640 El Jadida was under Spanish domination and then passed into Portuguese hands once more. A sultan of the present reigning dynasty, Sidi Mohammed ben Abdallah, succeeded in conquering the city in the year 1769; and it was rebuilt around 1815 by Moulay Abd er Rahman, who gave it its present name of New El Jadida. During the period of their protectorate, the French once again called it Mazagan until, after the 1956 proclamation of independence, it definitively regained its Arab name of El Jadida.

It is interesting to visit the picturesque old city, that is, the part created in the period of Portuguese domination, and transformed into a Jewish quarter; this visit starts from Place Mohammed V. Among other noteworthy monuments are the old church of the Assumption –a former theatre– overlooked on the left by the pentagonal minaret of the city's main mosque, and the old Portuguese cistern, a spacious underground room which is part of the old fortress built in 1514 and a remarkable piece of military engineering. Some sequences of the film «Othello» were shot here by the director Orson Welles. The Anjo bastion, overlooking the harbour, is another interesting sight.

Cistern dating to the 16th century.

Overall view with the Kechla Fortress, which now houses the National Museum of Ceramics.

A former Phoenician trading post according to the geographer Ptolemy, frequented by the Romans. This town was first given the name of *Asfi* by Ibn Khaldun. Its proximity to the Gantus mines has made Safi one of the chief phosphate processing and exporting centres in the entire world. This activity was boosted in 1965 with the opening of an industrial plant built with the technical co-operation of various European countries. Due to this important industry, the port of Safi, also well-known internationally because of its sardine fishing fleet, is the scene of the constant comings and goings of maritime traffic. The present site of the city of Safi was probably occupied by the ancient *Misokaras*, which Ptolomy situated between Cape Soleis and the mouth of the Fut. The city was mentioned, with the name Asfi, in the 11th century by the geographer El Bekri; and El Idrissi stated that it was a much frequented port in the 12th century. However, it was the historian Ibn Khaldun who –in the 14th century– made the most documented references to the fortified monastery known as Asfi. The port remained closed to European merchants until the 15th century; about 1480 commercial contacts were initiated

Minaret on the main mosque in Safi.

Dar Al Bahar fortress.

Traditional potter's kiln.

with Portugal. The governor of Mogador (Essaouira), Diego de Azambujo, and Admiral Garcia de Mello took the city in 1508 in the name of the king of Portugal, but the Portuguese abandoned the place in 1541.

Trade with Europe was intensified in the 17th century and Safi became one of the most important ports in Morocco. Towards the end of the 18th century Sidi Mohammed built a mosque and reinforced the city's defences. During the 19th century Safi underwent a period of decline, but it was reborn in the 20th, thanks to the industrialization brought about by its canning factories and the mining of phosphates. The most interesting monuments here include the ruins of Dar el Bahr –the castle by the sea–, built by the Portuguese at the beginning of the 16th century; Jama el Kebir –a large mosque–, the tomb of Sidi Abou Mohammed Salih –high dignitary of Safi–, the «Portuguese chapel», and the Kechla. Place de l'Independance is the city centre, and Rue du Souk the main throughfare in the old city, whose steep, narrow streets are particularly attractive.

Port of Essaouira, and the Medina.

The city of Essaouira appears as if by magic, surrounded by water, sand and flora, white and shining, its attractive silhouette standing between the sea and the dunes of the desert. The name Essaouira comes from *Al Souirah*, which in Arabic means «small fortress surrounded by walls». This was the name given to the city in the 18th century. Until Morocco's proclamation of Independence, it was called *Mogador*, a name that is possibly a translation to Spanish of the Berber word Amogdul (the protégé): the high dignitary of Essaouira, whose tomb is some three kilometres from the city, was called Sidi Mogdul.

The finding of remains of pottery on the islands in Essaouira bay testifies to the presence of the Phoenicians in the region from the 6th or 7th century B.C. onwards. It appears that during centuries the bay was barely frequented. However, the main island was once again populated at the end of the 1st century AD, this time on a permanent basis. The city

Port: fortress, or Sqala.

of Essaouira itself, sited on a promontory on terra firma, was apparently founded in the 18th century. Earlier, at the beginning of the 16th century, the Portuguese had built a fortress which was restored by Moulay Abd el Malek in 1628. The city was in fact founded by Sidi Mohammed Ben Abdallah, a member of the still reigning Alawid dynasty.
Essaouira, surrounded by high walls, is divided by means of interior walls into three clearly differentiated urban areas: the Medina, the Mellah and the Kasbah. There are many lovely gardens within the city, forming areas of delicious coolness.
The outstanding monuments here are the Porte de la Marine with the figure 1769 (the date of its construction) marked on the pediment, the Sqala in the harbour –an old battery whose cannons were made in Spain–, the Sqala in the Kasbah –an impressive platform some two hundred metres long– and the sanctuary of Moulay Abd el Kader el Jilali.
There is a splendid beach at Essaouira, with fine sand, where the climate is always mild because it is sheltered by the island in the bay.

Marine Gate and walls of Essaouira.

Beach of Essaouira.

The Jemaa El-Fna square at dusk.

Marrakesh is one of Morocco's imperial cities and the second oldest in the country. Known as «the pearl of the south», Marrakesh was founded by the Almoravids in the late 11th century. The most attractive place in the southern part of the country between the Atlas and the Sahara, it is an impressive sight to see this city from a distance surrounded by its palm groves, in the middle of the blazing hot plain of Haouz; in winter and in spring the peaks of nearby Mount Atlas are covered with snow.

It seems that the Berber Abou Bekr, the brave chief of an Almoravid tribe, was the founder of the city. His nephew Youssef ben Tachfin built a mosque and established himself in Marrakesh while Abou Bekr was in the Sahara fighting a group of rebels. Afterwards, when Abou Bekr came back, Youssef Ben Tachfin crossed the strait of Gibraltar and defeated the troops of Alphonse VI, enriching Marrakesh with his conquests and war trophies. The city developed considerably and became the most important trading centre in Morocco. In the

12th century, Abd el Mumin founded the Almohad dynasty. Marrakesh lived a period of great splendour under the Marinids, whose most famous Sultan was Ahmed el Mansour. On his death the city went through a period of decline. But Marrakesh regained its lost splendour, during the reign of the Alawid dynasty. Towards the end of the 19th century, Sultan Moulay Hassan enlarged the city, as did his son Moulay Abdal-Aziz; many of the buildings in it are owed to them.

Marrakesh is the great city of the Berbers. It has successfully preserved the pure mediaeval structure of the period of its foundation, the greater part of its architectural wealth dating from the period of the Almohads and the Saadis. The Almohads

Jemaa El-Fna square.

The Koutoubia Mosque.

The Koutoubia Mosque.

built the Koutoubia mosque, with its famous minaret, the Ben Youssef medersa (Moslem religious school) with its fine mosaic work, marble and valuable wood carvings; but it was the Saadis who had the honour of constructing the fascinating, impressive tombs containing the remains of the monarchs of this dynasty.

Other monuments of importance in Marrakesh include the Mouassîn and «Chrob ou Chouf» («drink and admire») fountains, the Bâb Aguenaou gate –in pure Almohad style– and the

The Medersa Ben Youssef: central courtyard.

Mosque where the Saadian Tombs lie.

The Saadian Tombs.

The 12th-century Bab Agnaou Gate.

The great courtyard in El Bahia Palace.

Interior of El Bahia Palace.

19th-century Bahia Palace, with its splendid gardens.
The Dar Si Saïd Museum is particularly important: situated in a palace built in 1900, which in 1914 became the residence of the chiefs of the Marrakesh region. After being restored in 1932 it was converted into the Museum of Moroccan Art, where valuable Berber jewellery is on show, together with a collection of velvet caftans embroidered with golden thread, ceramics, tapestries, carpets, tooled leather objects, weapons

Dar Si Said Palace, which now houses the Museum of Moroccan Art.

from many different places and mosaics.
Marrakesh, with its colourful, dynamic markets and extraordinary wealth of handicrafts, is one of the most attractive cities in the whole of Morocco. It can be said that it is a city that has kept its heritage of folklore in all its fascinatingly original richness. The Marrakesh Festival is usually celebrated in the month of May; the highest point of picturesque splendour is the daily folklore celebration

Medina: souk.

Avenue of Mohammed V (Gueliz), Boulevard Al Yarmouk and the Royal Palace.

Majorelle Garden.

There are in Marrakesh many riads, mansions whose rooms are organised around a central courtyard.

centred on Place Jemaa el Fna, the veritable heart of the city. The most important avenues in the city are the Avenue Mohammed V, Avenue Hassan II, Avenue El Menara, Avenue de France, Avenue du Président Kennedy, Avenue des Nations Unies, Boulevard de Safi and Rue El Irak.

Place Jemaa el Fna, already mentioned, is the nerve-centre of Marrakesh and is near the Bahia Palace, the tombs of the Sultans of the Saadi dynasty, the Koutoubia and Bâb Doukkala mosques and the medersa of Ben Youssef. A little further away are the ruins of El Badii royal palace, built in the 16th century, the present Royal Palace and two wonderful parks: the Majorelle Garden, created in the 1930s; and La Menara, laid out in the 19th century.

Northwest of the medina is the Palmeraie neighbourhood, a vast oasis populated by more

Jemaa el Fna square.

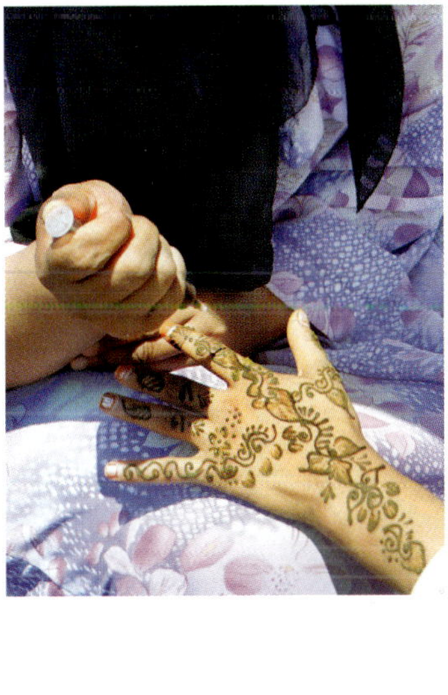

Menara Gardens.

El-Badii Palace.

than one hundred thousand palm trees. Palmeraie is today an area occupied by many hotels and luxury residences. Other recommended excursions include visits to the Kasbah at Tamesloht, **Oumnass**, the "Golden Town", the **Ouzoud** waterfalls, the natural bridge at **Imi n'Ifri** and the lake at **Ait Aadel**.

Folklore performance in the Palmeraie neighbourhood.

The Ouzoud Falls, where the river waters plunge into a green abyss, 100 m high, a sight 150 km from Marrakesh.

Ouarzazate: Taourirt Kasbah.

An important communications centre and the point at which the Draa, Dades and Sous valleys meet, Ouarzazate has knowingly made the most of its privileged location to become a modern town which each year attracts a great many tourists. Today it is the administrative capital of a province of the same name and the site of an international airport. With 71,000 inhabitants, the town's principal activities also include trading and tra-

Taourirt Kasbah.

Partial views of the Taourirt Kasbah. ▶

ditional handcrafts. The latter of the two is centred on the creation of beautiful ceramic ware and carpets decorated with geometric motifs made by true craftsmen.
The architecture in Ouarzazate generally displays a great uniformity further accentuated by its red toned buildings. Its most unique and beautiful building is the Taourirt Kasbah, whose construction began in the mid-18th century. This magnificent

place is where the pasha of Marrakech once lived, master of the Glaoui. The Glaoui was the most powerful of all the Berber tribes in the High-Atlas. The Taourirt Kasbah is in fact a small town constructed with military precision in which the simplicity and austerity of its adobe facades contrast with the delicately decorated interiors. Particularly spectacular is the favoured one's bedroom and the dining room, both with exquisite stucco ornamentation on cedar wood. In the Kasbah, criss-crossed by numerous backstreets, there also exists a mellah, or Jewish quarter.
Another great attraction in Ouarzazate are the **Atlas Corporation film studios**, which are open to the public and which even has a Film Museum where visitors can admire sets and costumes used in many films partly shot here, such as *Gladiator, Kundun, The Mummy* and *Kingdom of Heaven*. The studios and the wonderful landscape around here, have also been used as locations for such well-known series as *Prison Break, Vikings* and *Game of Thrones*.
In the environs of Ouarzazate are more Kasbahs and Ksour that reflect the political and economic importance that Glaoui once enjoyed. The best conserved include Kasbah of **Tifoultoute**, just 8 kilometres to the west; the Kasbah of **Teloeut**, 77 kilometres to the northwest, and, especially, the **Aït-Ben-Haddou** ksar, 30 kilometres along the road to Telouet, listed as a World Heritage Site by UNESCO in 1987. Heading southeast for 70 kilometres, and just after passing the city of **Agdz**, the landscape changes dramatically, tinged with the green of the oases which mark out the course of the river Draa. We have just entered the **Draa Valley**, a natural expanse dotted with numerous Ksar or fortified settlements which extends as far as the town of Zagora. The Draa is born near to Ouarzazate, fed by the waters which descend the High Atlas Mountains from the rivers Dades and Ouarzazate. The river's course initially flows along a narrow open gorge in the Sarhro massif to later run more than 200 kilometres

The Aït Ben Haddou Kasbah near Ouarzazate.

The Draa Valley.

along the plain which extends from Agdz. The main crop in the valley are date palms. The valley's inhabitants, essentially Arabs and sedentary Berbers, suffered hostility from the desert nomads for years. For this reason they decided to protect themselves constructing defence enclosures known by the name of Ksour or, in the singular, Ksar. Of the many Ksour and Kasbahs in the Draa Valley we can highlight particularly, and from north to south, **Tamnougalt** (ancient Amazigh capital), **Timidarte, Oulad Othmane, Tinzouline, Tissergate** and **Zagora**.

Ksar of Tamnougalt.

Partial view of the Taroudant city walls.

Details of Taroudant.

This charming city was once the capital of the Sous region, a large plain bathed in sunlight gilding the hillsides and enriching the earth. Taroudant is famous for its unusual, artistic, craftwork. The carved stones, Berber jewels and old weapons are much appreciated.

Taroudant has a long history. At the beginning of the 11th century the city was the capital of a Shiah principality, established with the help of the Fatimids of Ifrikuiya. In 1056 it fell into the hands of the Almoravids but gained its independence during the Almohad period, under the leadership of the Yedder family. After being destroyed in the 14th century, the city's fortifications were rebuilt and it became the metropolitan city of Sous. In the 16th century, after regaining its independence, Taroudant enjoyed a period of splendour and was an important centre for trade with the Sudan. Later, in the time of Mohammed Ibn Abd er Rahman, the city became the centre of resistance against the Portuguese who had settled in Agadir. After the Portuguese fortress of Cap Rhir was taken, Taroudant lost its status as the Saadi capital, until Mohammed ech Cheikh conquered Marrakesh. Because of the support it had lent to the cause of Ahmed Ibn Mahrez in the 17th century, the Alawid sultan Moulay Ismaïl conquered Taroudant in 1687. Towards the end of the 19th century it became a centre of intrigue against the central authority until 1913.

Its narrow winding streets and narrow Place d'Assarag flanked by picturesque markets, lend the city of Taoroudant an enchanting air for the tourist. The city has a distinctive appearance, surrounded by crenellated walls, gardens, olive trees and palms.

Tiout.

Among the possible excursions from Taroudant, particularly interesting is the visit to the Kasbah of **Tiout**, a magnificent viewpoint over the Souss Valley, and to **Taliouine**, which also has an interesting Kasbah and city and is known, above all, as the largest centre for saffron production in Morocco.

Taliouine: crocus flower and kasbah.

Tafraoute.

The scenery here is of exceptional beauty. An enormous elemental mass of rounded red rocks that seem to keep their balance by means of some strange, complicated mechanism, it looks like a fantastic kasbah of ochre-red walls surmounted by white battlements contrasting with the green tones of the vegetation: an original, harmonious picture. Mount Tafraoute sometimes takes on amethyst tones and the summits are as if crowned with bold tones that dazzle the visitor. This little mountain is situated in the west of the Anti-Atlas, between Agadir and Tiznit. The excursion to Tafraoute is one of the most delightful ones that can be undertaken in the south of Morocco. In this area, we can discover Berber culture in its valleys, villages and oases. It is as if time had stood still, for the day-to-day life of the people here seems totally unaffected by mass tourism.

Typical houses in Tafraoute.

The red mosque of Adaï, near Tafroute.

Rocks on the Tafraoute route, painted by the Belgian artist Jean Vérame in 1984.

Tineghir.

Berber jewel.

The oasis of Tineghir, famous for its palm trees and many kasbahs, is one of the largest and loveliest in Morocco. It abounds in luxuriant vegetation and is situated close to the Todgha. The town is a former military post situated on the route from Ouarzazate to Ksar es Souk (today Errachidia), and is terraced around a hill on top of which stands the old castle of the Glaoui (an old pasha in Morocco) as well as the Hôtel Sagro. The visitor can enjoy broad, beautiful panoramas from the terraces of Glaoui palace and the Hôtel Sagro.

One of Tineghir's outstanding tourist attractions –apart from the delightful excursions that can be taken from the oasis– is the quality of the Berber jewellery in silver and other metals made in the locality.

One trip that no visitor to Tinerhir should miss, are the **Todra or Todgha Gorges**, just 10

Oasis of Tineghir.

The Todra Gorges.

kilometres to the northwest. Here, the river runs between rock walls rising to over 300 metres in height, with a width of just 20 metres in some sections. Another example of the natural wonders here are the **Dades Gorges**, 70 kilometres to the west. The route along this canyon, which presents difficulties even for those driving land-rovers, reveals a series of narrow valleys eroded by the River Dades as it opened up its path through the High Atlas Mountains. Scattered over the region, moreover, are the ruins of ancient Kasbahs and Ksour. The most outstanding include those of **Tamellalt** and those of the **Kalaat m'Gouna** oasis, also known as the Valley of Roses.

Kasbah and crafts for sale on the Dades Gorges route.

Dades Gorge: the road known as Tissadrine ("The Serpent").

Ancient Kasbah at the Kalaat M'Gouna oasis.

A view of Agadir from the Kasbah.

An important sea resort, Agadir is a city of considerable attraction for the tourist as, apart from the privilege of its ideal climate, it has a magnificent beach, the longest in all Morocco.

Agadir is of very ancient origins and many authors have identified it with the ancient port of *Russadir* mentioned by Polybius. Apparently the Carthaginian admiral Hannon visited Russadir. In 1505 the Portuguese João Lopes de Sequeira built a small fort known as Santa Cruz de Cap Rhir close to what is now Agadir, at Aït Funti. Eight years later this fort was sold to the king of Portugal. From 1531 onwards Mohammed ech Cheikh established a military base at Tamragh, some twelve kilometres away, which fell into Moroccan hands on 12th March 1541 after several previous attacks. Agadir played an important part as a

Marina Agadir residential area.

Kasbah or Agadir Oufella.

commercial centre in the 17th century, with Denmark gaining the monopoly of its trade in 1751. Sultan Sidi Mohammed ben Abdallah halted Agadir's commercial activities so as to stimulate the development of trade at Essaouira. Agadir underwent a period of decline throughout the 19th century,

Beach, Marina Agadir resort and, looking down on all this, the Kasbah.

The Loubnan Mosque.

but in the 20th it once more became a flourishing city. In 1960, Agadir was almost completely destroyed by an earthquake that killed around 15,000 people, a third of the population at that time. The city was rebuilt immediately afterwards according to a new urban design characterised by wide avenues and squares. Today, Agadir is not only one

Town Hall of Agadir.

Boulevard of Mohammed V.

Mohammed V Mosque: main entrance.

Medina Coco Polizzi.

of the country's main tourist resorts thanks to its beaches, but also has the most important port zone in Morocco, with two ports, one commercial and one a pleasure port, the latter housed in the residential and shopping area known as Marina Agadir.

The most attractive feature of Agadir is its Kasbah, a veritable eyrie perched 236 metres above sea level: built in the year 1540 by Mohammed ech Cheikh as a starting point from which to launch his offensive against the Portuguese fortress, and restored in 1752, this is a fine vantage point with a magnificent view of the sea.

Other interesting monuments of thc city include the mosques of Mohammed V and Loubnane, the modern rationalist-style buildings housing City Hall (by Le Corbusier) and the Post Office (by the architect Jean-François Zevaco) and, in the suburbs, Medina Coco Polizzi, a medina created in 1992 by the Italian

Tourist train.

The argan tree, very common in Agadir region.

Argan oil production.

Taghazout beach.

artist of the same name, using traditional Berber techniques. Another recommended attraction is the Souk al-Had, the biggest urban souk in Africa, with around 6,000 shops organised by sector, visited daily by an average of 40,000 people.
As for excursions from Agadir, **Paradise Valley**, some 33 kilometres from the city, is a canyon on the Tamraght River with many natural swimming pools and spectacular waterfalls.

Waterfalls of Imouzzer Ida Ou Tanane, in Paradise Valley. ▶

This is a picturesque town located some 100 kilometres from Agadir, and famous for its craft work. The worked Berber silver jewellery and decoratively encrusted weapons are the typical products of Tiznit and constitute a great tourist attraction.

Tiznit was founded in 1882, by Moulay el Hassan during a military expedition. The city then became an important trading centre. In 1919, the city was occupied by the French, who stayed until 1956, when Morocco was proclaimed independent.

Tiznit is an unusually attractive place, with a mosque surrounded by palm trees with a minaret in Sudanese style, the Medina and Jewish quarter, and its winding streets where there are many jewellers' shops.

Interesting excursions can be made from Tiznit, to the Anti-Atlas and **Foum el Hassan, Akka, Tata** and **Foum Zguid**, localities with luxuriant palm trees close to the immense Sahara desert.

A trip to **Goulimine** is also interesting: the market here is a particularly attractive spot for the Saharan camel-drivers, being the first of a series of

The Great Mosque in Tiznit.

Goulimine: jewellers stands.

Jeweller's market: coffer.

The souk in Goulimine attracts many tribes from all around.

oases in the foothills of the Bani mountains.

Along the coast of Tiznit are new residential areas that have given considerable boost to development in the region. The nearest is the population of **Aglou** with its beach, **Sidi Moussa**. Due to the frequent high wind here, swimming in the open sea is not recommended, but the beach is a veritable haven for lovers of paragliding.

Goulimine: gateway to the desert.

Goulimine: camel market.

Ksar Tafnidilt, near Tan-Tan.

Legzira beach.

Mosque of Laayoune.

Lying the southernmost part of Morocco, flanked by the Atlantic Ocean on the one side and Mauritania on the other, the Saharan provinces (or Western Sahara) cover an area around 1,000 kilometres long by a width varying between 280 and 500 kilometres. The Saharan landscape is characterised by the capricious forms of dunes running through which it is not unusual to find old paths used long ago by the desert caravans, as well as tiny streams which rarely reach the nearby sea. Since 1976, when Spain granted Morocco sovereignty over the region, the population of the Saharan provinces has grown steadily, due to a large entent to the process of modernisation undertaken since.

Laayoune, the largest centre of population, combines the legacy of its Spanish past with more recent architectural and works and town planning developments sponsored by the Moroccan authorities. Other local attractions include the holy city of **Smara**, 200 kilometres east of El Aaiún, where we find the ruins of the old alcazaba fortress and the mosque built when the city was founded in 1888, and several towns on or very close to the coast. These are, from north to south: **Mirleft, Legzira** and **Sidi Ifni**, all with spectacular beaches that are frequented by surfers due to the strong winds in the area; **Tan-Tan**, near the Ksar of Tafnidilt; and the fishing villages **of Tarfaya** and **Dakhla**, the latter 500 kilometres from Laayoune and 600 kilometres from Tarfaya.

Rissani.

To the north and east of Tinerhir extends the province of Er Rachidia, which encompasses various oases on the banks of the *ouadis* Ziz, Guir and Ghris, one of the more outstanding being that of **Tafilalt**, near to **Erfoud**. On account of its geographical situation, this region has been the historical crossroads between the imperial cities and Morocco's great south, its tourist attractions are today both multiple and varied. Cultural tourism is clearly evident in the architectural heritage and development of the ksour and kasbahs and also in the wealth of styles and customs from the province's different tribes, all of which have enriched the great Tafilalt civilisation, seat of the Moroccan dynasty in which the lost city of **Sijilmassa**, its main trading centre, played a decisive role in the Saharan caravan routes. The ruins of Sijilmasa lie 2 kilometres from the city of **Rissani**, which replaced the former as the main commercial centre in the region. Besides a large souk, the attractions

Camp in the Erg Chebbi Dunes.

Every year, in September, a traditional "moussem" takes place in Ilmilchil. The "moussem" is an assembly of Nomad tribes, who meet to rekindle family ties and agree marriages between families.

in Rissani also include a 17th-century Kasbah.

The province is, on the other hand, famous for its festivals, especially the October Date Festival, in **Erfoud**, an event in which there is no shortage of traditional camel races, and for the organisation of moussems such as the internationally famed betrothal moussem, which takes place in **Imilchil**, in September. The Saharan landscape to the south of the province, with its oases offering relaxation and shade, constitutes another original tourist attraction ideally suited to lovers of adventure and nature. To discover this fascinating world of sand dunes, excursions are organised by various agencies either with all terrain vehicles or by camel.

The Erg Chebbi Dunes.

The **Erg Chebbi** dunes, near **Merzouga**, are particularly attractive and much frequented by visitors from around the world who come to take sand baths, which are particularly recommended for those who suffer from rheumatism.
Another type of bath, containing thermal waters, can likewise be enjoyed in this region. Worthy of note are the thermal springs at Hammat Moulay Ali Cherif, Hammat Moulay Hachem and the Blue Spring (Source Bleue) in **Meski**, all in the **Valley of Ziz**. This magnificent green valley, which extends between the High-Atlas Mountains and the boundaries of the Sahara, conceals other natural marvels such as the **Ziz Gorge**, where the Ziz *ouadi* makes its way squeezed between high crags, along which extends a green fringe of palm trees.
To the northeast of the province, the High Atlas Mountains, some with summits more than 3,200 metres in altitude, provide the perfect opportunity to practice sports such as alpinism, trekking, horse riding, hunting and fishing.

The Blue Fountain, in Meski.

The Ziz Gorge.

From its ideal position on a strategic amphitheatre of hills, this attractive white city stands opposite the straits of Gibraltar, its excellent port links Europe and Africa by sea. Tangier is a city with a distinct personality, the past and the present mingling harmoniously in its appearance: typically Moroccan charm juxtaposed with the functional design of the large, modern buildings. The origins of ancient *Tingi* are shrouded in legend; ac-

The Tangier medina.

Streets of the medina.

The Kasbah walls.

The Kasbah Mosque.

Sidi Boubaid Mosque.

cording to Hellenic mythology, the city of Tangier was founded by the famous king Antheus. During the period of Roman domination it became the capital of the province of Mauritania Tingitana. In 429 the city was occupied by the Vandals, led by Genseric. Later it became a dependency of the Byzantine Empire. It was from Tangier that the ships under Tarik set sail in 711 to begin the conquest of Spain. After the passage of the Almoravids and the Almohads, the city suffered different adventures; it was conquered by the Portuguese in 1471 and reconquered by Moulay Ismail at the end of

The “Petit Socco” square.

The “Grand Socco” square.

Cape Espartel lighthouse.

the 17th century. After having enjoyed a special status for many years, as a consequence of the Algeciras Conference in 1906, Tangier was definitively incorporated into the kingdom of Morocco when the latter became independent in 1956. The city has an unusually attractive atmosphere: the evocative Great Socco and Small Socco (markets), the gardens of the Sultan, with the dominating presence of the Great Mosque, the mysterious, white, zigzagging structure of the Kasbah with the old palace founded by Moulay Ismail containing the Moroccan Art Museum and the Archaeological Museum, the Dar ech Cherâ (Moslem law courts) and Bâb el Assa gate make up a varied scene full of authentic Arab vitality, connected via Rue d'Italie and Rue Ben Raisoul with the dynamic modern city with its fine avenues, restaurants, hotels, magnificent sports facilities and lovely beach.
Various interesting excursions can be undertaken from the city: the **Cap Spartel** itinerary, where there are magnificent views of the sea and the mountains; the **grottoes of Hercules**; **Cotta**, a former Punic and Roman trading post; **Cap Malabata** –attractive places such as these follow one upon another along the

Sea mouth of the Caves of Hercules, its silhouette reminding us of a map of Africa.

The Medina of Asilah: partial view, and mural painting.

road skirting the bay– and the city of **Asilah**. Situated 46 kilometres from Tangier, Asilah is one of the most beautiful coastal resorts in the country. Its charming medina is enclosed by excellently-conserved walls built by the Portuguese in the 15th century. An unusual attraction here are the mural paintings that adorn the exterior of several houses, painted by artists that visit the town, and a work of flagstone paving made by local artists. Visitors to Asilah will also find magnificent beaches.

Tetouan: Feddane square, which links the old town to the new city.

An important city on the hill of Dersa, only sixty kilometres from Tangier, Tétouan is surrounded by lovely countryside with many gardens watered by the Martil. This is one of the most genuinely Arab cities in the Mediterranean area of Morocco. Founded at the beginning of the 14th century by the Marinid sultan Abu Thabit, Tétouan is situated near the ancient *Tamuda*. The city soon became highly prosperous, but Henry III of Castile destroyed it in 1399, killing half its inhabitants and deporting the rest to Europe. After being repopulated at the beginning of the 16th century, it became an active trading centre. After several changes of fortune, Tétouan enjoyed a period of splendour in the 18th century, during the reign of Moulay Ismail. The city was occupied by the Spaniards in the middle of the 19th century; and became definitively incorporated into the kingdom of Morocco in 1956.

The Bab el-Oqla Gate.

Tétouan displays attractive city walls, many mosques (Sidi es Saldi is the most outstanding), picturesque streets with delightful archways over them, Bâb er Remous gate (from which there is a fine panoramic view of the valley of the river Martil), the Royal Palace, and the Al-Andalus-style houses in the medina. The nearby Roman ruins at Tamuda are also of interest. UNESCO listed Tetouan's old town, or Medina, as a World Heritage site in 1997.

Tétouan furthermore offers the splendid beach of the river Martil, some twenty-five kilometres long.

There are two important museums in Tétouan: the Archaeological Museum (with interesting

Details of the medina.

The Medina Mosque.

Sidi Saidi Mosque.

Roman pieces, fragments of Iberian and Greco-Punic pottery, jewels, coins and the two large mosaics discovered at Lixus, depicting the Three Graces and an infant Bacchus) and the Moroccan Folklore and Art Museum.

There are some interesting excursions from here, to **El Ksar es Séghir**, with its old Portuguese citadel, on the Atlantic coast; and the spa town of **Al Hoceima**, on the Mediterranean coast.

Royal Palace: main entrance.

Chefchaouen: overall view.

A charming little city at 610 metres above sea level, Chéfchaouen is defended by imposing rocks and is extremely picturesque in appearance. Its white buildings and many green spaces and fountains make it a real garden city. Founded in the late 15th century by Moulay Ben Rachid, it still preserves from its past glory a fortress with a mediaeval turret. The main points of interest are the Medina, with its one-storey white and blue washed houses; Uta el-Hammam square beside the fortress walls; and the Great Mosque, which dates to the 15th century. There are also half a dozen mosques and many sanctuaries.

This is a city with a great future in tourism: an ideal starting point for excursions in the Rif mountains that line the Mediterranean seaboard from the strait of Gibraltar to the mouth of the Moulouya on the Morocco-Algeria frontier.

Blue and white are the main colours in the Medina at Chéfchaouen.

Uta el Hamman square, the fortress, and the Great Mosque.

RABAT
N
OCÉAN ATLANTIQUE
KÉNITRA
BAB CHAFAA
SIDI BEN ACHIR
BORJ NORD-OUEST
BAB SEBTA
ROUTE DE KÉNITRA
AV. YACOUB AL MANSOUR
BOU TOUIL
GRANDE MOSQUÉE
SIDI ABDALLAH BEN HASSOUN
SALÉ
JAMAA SIDI ALI
BAB SEBTA
GRANDE MOSQUÉE
SOUIKA
SIDI AHMED HAYI
ABOU YOUSSEF AL MRINI
FONDOUK ASKOUR
DAR RAY
BAB JDID
BAB FÈS
ROUTE N°1
MEKÍNEZ
CHARI AHMED BEN ABOUD
AV. DE LA PLAGE
SALÉ
BAB MRISA
ATELIER DE TAPIS
KASBAH DES OUDAÏAS
PORTE DES OUDAÏAS
MUSÉE DES OUDAÏAS
OUED BOU REGREG
PONT MOULAY HASSAN
OUED BOU REGREG
TARIK AL-MARSA
BOULEVARD AL-ALOU
BOULEVARD MOKHTAR GAZOULET
BAB EL-ALOU
PL. ECH-CHOUADA
MÉDINA
CONSULS
MELLAH
SIDI FATAH
AV. MOHAMMED V
GRANDE MOSQUÉE
BAB AL-MELLAH
MOSQUÉE MOULAY EL MEKKI
PL. SIDI MAKHLOUF
BOULEVARD HASSAN II
BOULEVARD ABI REGREG
TOUR HASSAN
BOULEVARD ARRAHIBAH
SOUIKA
MOULAY SLIMAN
ABDELKRIM AL KHATTABI
AV. AL MOUKAOUAMA
AV. MISIR
BOULEVARD HASSAN II
JARDIN TRIANGLE DE VUE
PL. MELILVA
MELIVA
MOULAY ISMAIL
ABDELMOUMEN
AL-MARINIYINE
AV. AL-ALAOUIYINE
MAUSOLÉE DE MOHAMMED V
AV. MOSTAFA E.S.-SAID
B. ROUDANI
OCÉAN
BAB EL-HAD
AV. AL MAGHRIB AL ARABI
THÉÂTRE MOHAMED V
AV. ALLAL BEN
P. LUMUMBA
CHELLAH
MOURABITINE
AV. AL-ALAOUNNE
TUNIS
AV. JEAN JAURÈS
AV. JEAN JAURÈS
SOEKAMO
PL. AL JOULANE
AV. MOHAMMED V
ST. PIERRE
PL. MOULAY AL HASSAN
AL-JAZAIR
PL. ABRAHAM LINCOLN
EL HACHIMI
AL MESTARI
AV. SIDI MOHAMMED BEN ABDALLAH
KEBIRAT
AV. DE MADAGASCAR
AV. TONKIN
AVENUE HASSAN II
LES ORANGERS
AV. IBN TOUMERT
GARE RABAT-VILLE
PL. J. ASSOUNA
AV. MOULAY HASSAN
CHELLAH
AV. FES
BOULEVARD TARIQ IBN ZIYAD
AV. DE MEKNÈS
OMAR SLAOUI
AV. MOHAMMED ZERQTOUNI
AV. AL-MARRAKCHI
AV. AL GHAZZALI
AV. A.
AV. PASTEUR
BAB ER ROUAH
PL. EN-NASR
MUSÉE ARCHÉOLOGIQUE
MOSQUÉE AS SOUNNA
PRESIDENT ROOSEVELT
AV. MARRAKECH
SALINES
PL. BAB TAMESNA
AVENUE EN-NASR
MINISTÈRES ET AMBASSADES
AV. MOHAMMED V
BOULEVARD MOUSSA IBN NOSSAIR
PL. MOHAMMED ZERQTOUNI
AV. IBN AL-OUAZZANE
JARDIN D'ESSAI
OQBAH
AV. IBN KHALDOUN
MÉCHOUAR
AV. YACOUB AL-MANSOUR
RUINES DE SALA
MUSÉE DES SCIENCES DE LA TERRE
AV. IBN HAMZ
AV. IBN BATOUTA
AHL FAS
NECROPOLE CHELLAH
ROUTE A CASABLANCA
STADE MUNICIPAL
BAB ZAËR
AV. INNAOUEN
PL. IBN YACINE
AV. INNAOUEN
UNIVERSITÉ
MÉCHOUAR
CHELLAH
MOHAMMED TRIKI
OQBAH
AV. AL-ABTAL
BOULEVARD AD DOUSTOUR
AV. AMIR FAL OULD OUMEIR
AV. OMAR IBN AL KHATTAB
AV. OUMAM AL-MOUTTA
PALAIS DU ROI
MÉCHOUAR
GARE RABAT-AGDAL
RAHMAN AL GHAFIKI
AV. AL-ABTAL
AV. JOHN KENNEDY
AGDAL
AV. FRANSA
0
750
MEKNÈS, OUED ZEM

CASABLANCA
OCÉAN ATLANTIQUE
DARSE COMMERCIALE
DARSE DU TOURISME
GARE DE CHARGEMENT
QUAI MULAY YUSUF
QUAI DU COMMERCE
LA MOSQUÉE HASSAN II
SOUR IDID
BD. SIDI MOHAMMED BEN ABDALLAH
BD. SOUR DJEDID
R. BIN EL QUIDANE
AQUARIUM
R. BISSON
R. ADAM
R. DE TIZNIT
R. FLAUBERT
R. LA BOETIE
R. JULES MAURAN
RUE CUVIER
BOULEVARD MOULAY
BOULEVARD EL HANK
R. DIDEROT
R. DE GOULMINA
BD. DE BORDEAUX
R. DE L'ALMA
R. MONTGOLFIER
R. DE CAMP. TURPIN
BOURGOGNE OUEST
RUE DU DOCTEUR GIEURE
R. DE L'AVENIR
BOULEVARD ZIRAOUI
MEDINA
SANCTUAIRE SIDI EL-KAIROUANI
MOSQUÉE ECH-CHLEUH
BAB JÉDID
VIEILLE MELLAH
BD. TAHAR
EL ALAOUI
BOUL DES ALMOHADES
ECH CHLEUH
MOSQUÉE DAR EL MAJZEN
BD. FÉLIX HOUPHOUËT-BOIGNY
GARE DE CHEMIN DE FER, DU PORT
BOULEVARD MOULAY ABDERRAHMAN
RUE ZAID OU HMAD
R. DE GOULMINA
R.DES ANGLAIS
R. VERLET HANUS
YOUSSEF ER RAHAL
AV. DE L'ARMÉE ROYALE
CENTRE
PLACE MOHAMMED V
PLACE OUED EL MAKHAZINE
R.F. ET M. GUEDEJ
BD. D'ANFA
LUSITANIA
UNIVERSITÉ
CTM-LN BUS
R. ALLAL BEN ABDALLAH
BD. MOHAMMED V
BD. HASSAN SEGHIR
RUE DE TOURS
RUE DE TOUTON
AV. DE L'ARMÉE ROYALE (des FAR)
PLACE MIRABEAU
AV. PASTEUR
R. KARATCHI
PLACE N. PAQUET
AV. MOULAY HASSAN Ier
BOUL. DE PARIS
IDRISS LAHRIZI
MOULAY ABDALLAH
PLACE D'AKNOUL
SIDI BELYOUT
PLACE 20 AOUT
RUE MOHAMMED DIOURI
R. DES OULED ZIANE
BD. DE LA RESISTANCE
BD. MOHAMMED V
PLACE EL-YASSIR
GARE
RUE DE PROVINS
BD. EMILE ZOLA
POSTE
THEATRE
PLACE DES NATIONS UNIES
BOUL. RACHIDI
CATHEDRALE DU SACRE-COEUR
AVENUE HASSAN II
TRIBUNAL
R. PRINCE
AV. LALLA YACOUL
RUE DE STRASBOURG
MOHAMMED SMIHA
RUE BASCUNAN
RUE KHOURIBGA
ROND-POINT DAKAR
BD. ABDELLAH BEN YACINE
PREFECTURE
BD. DU 11 JANVIE
PLACE DE L'UNITÉ AFRICAINE
STADE
BOULEVARD MOULAY YOUSSEF
R. MOSTAPHA EL-MAANI
LIBERTÉ
EL-MESKINI
ER-RAHAL
PLACE VICTOIRE
RUE E. BARATHON
R. C. PUISSESSEAU
R. D'EVIAN
BOUL IBN TACHFINE
PARC DE LA LIGUE ARABE
R. OMAR SLAOUI
O.N.M.T.
R. HADJ
AV. MERS SULTAN
RUE DE NANCY
AMAR RIFFI
BD. D'ALSACE
BD. LAHCEN OU IDER
R. CANIZARÈS
RESISTANCE
RUE DE LIBOURNE
BD. DE LA GIRONDE
RUE DE BAZAS
GAUTIER
BOULEVARD
R. OLLIER
R. DE LA PAIX
R. MESSAOUDI
R. D'ASSAS
RUE MOUSSA BEN NOUSSAIR
AV. HASSAN SOUKTANI
RUE JEAN JAURÈS
GALILÉE
R. BUFFON
EL-MASSIRA EL KHADRA
TWIN CENTER
R. DE MONT CENIS
POLICE
RUE DU CADET LAMY
BOULEVARD BRAHIM ROUDANI
ZERKTOUNI
MARIF
R. DU MARCHÉ
R. DU MONT DORE
R. DU JURA
RUE DES FAUCILLES
R. D'AUVERGNE
R. DU PRIVOUX
MERS SULTAN
RUE DE REIMS
R. DE CALAIS
ROND-POINT HASSAN II
BD. MOHAMMED
ZERKTOUNI
ROND-POINT D'EUROPE
NOTRE-DAME DE LOURDES
PLACE LEMAIGRE DUBREUIL
ROUTE DE MÉDIOUNA
RUE DES QUINCONCES
GIRONDE
RUE D'IFNI
PLACE HAMIDOU EL-WATANI
BD. DE LONDRES
R. DE CONSTANTINOPLE
RUE OMAR EL IDRISSI
R. HADJ AMAR RIFFI
R. IBN TOUMERT
PALAIS ROYAL
GARE DE CHEMIN DE FER
BD. VICTOR HUGO
R. DE L'ÉCOLE INDUSTRIELLE
R. BULLET
HOPITAUX
R. CLAUDE LORRAIN
R. ERAZI
PALMIER
R. MEISSONNIER
RUE CHARLES LEBRUN
RUE EL-MOUTANABI
RUE PIERRE PUGET
BOULEVARD ABDELMOUMEN
RUE DU DOCTEUR BRAUN
RUE PINEL
CEUTA
PARC MURDOCH
AV. DU 2 MARS
BD. VICTOR HUGO
HABOUS
R. AHMED EL-FIGUIGUI
PL. MOULAY YOUSSEF
MAHAKMA DU PACHA
MEDINA NUEVA
R. DU RIFFI
ROUTE D'EL-JADIDA
R. G. SAND
R. DE ROUEN
DANTON

MEKNES
BAB EL-BARDAYN
MOSQUÉE EL-BARDAYN
BAB TIZIMI
MAUSOLÉE DE SIDI MOHAMMED BEN AÏSSA
BAB ES-SIBA
BAB JIDID
KUBBA DE MULAY AHMED EL UAZZANI
MEDINA
PARC EL-HABUL
BOUL. EL-HABOUL
RUE EL-ANDLAOUS
RUE EL-MRINYINE
R. OKBA BEN NAFII
RUE YOUGOSLAVIE
BD. EL MOURABITINE
RUE OMAR ABDELAZIZ
CITÉ NO
RUE MANSOUR ED-DAHBI
EL-MOUQAOUAMA
AV. EL-AMIR
MOULAY
PL. ABDELAZIS BEN IDRISSS
RUE PASTEUR
PL. MAURITANIA
RUE FERHAT HACHAD
RUE OMAR EL-MOUTANABI
AVENUE HASSAN II
RUE GHANDI
RUE D'ACCRA
AVENUE 11 JANVIER
LA POSTE PLACE
CITÉ DE VILLE
ADMINISTRATIVE
TRIBUNAL
IDRISS
AV. MOULAY ISMAÏL
AV. BENGAZI
CARREFOUR BOU MAYR
ESPLANADE DE LA FOIRE
AVENUE DES
ROUTE BOU MAYR
RUE DES MOULINS
RUE ROUAMZINE
DAR EL-MANSOUR
MEDERSA BOU INANIA
GRAND MOSQUÉE
KAYSARIA
MEDERSA FILALA
R. DU SOUK EN-NEJJARIN
R. DU SOUK ES-SEBBAT
MOSQUÉE EN-NEJJARIN
RUE EL-HANAYA
R. DU SOUK BEJARIN
RUE DES SERAIRIA
CIMETIÈRE DE LALLA JIMELIA
BAB BERRIMA
DAR JAMAÏ
R. DAR SEMEN
PLACE EL-HEDIM
PLACE LALLA AOUDA
MOSQUÉE DE LALLA AUDA
BAB EL-MANSOUR
DAR KEBIRA
BAB BOU AMAR
BOLEVARD ABDERRAHMANE BEN ZIDANE
BAB SIDI AMAR EL HASSANI
RUE SIDI AMAR EL-HASSANI
BOULEVARD EL-MERS
SIDI AMAR
AV. DU MELLAH
RUE SEKKAKIN
MOSQUÉE BAB BERRIMA
BERRIMA
BAB EL-MELLAH
MELLAH ANCIENNE
BAB EL JEMIS
BD. ES-SALAM
BAB JAMA EN-NOUAR
KOUBBET EL-KHIYATIN
MAUSOLÉE DE MULAY ISMAÏL
BAB MOULAY ISMAÏL
BAB ER-RIH
GOLF
RUE IBN ZAIDOUN
MELLAH NOUVELLE
RUE DE PALESTINE
RUE EL QODS
RUE MOUSTAWCAF
BORDJ EL-MA
UADI B
DAR EL-MAKHZEN
MEXUAR
BAB EL QARI
CITÉ IMPERIALE
BAB NAOURA
KASBA
HA
DJ MACHOQQ
BENI MHAHHAD
ETANG D'AGDAL
DAR EL-MA
HÉRI ES-SOUANI
SBATA
TOUARGA
DAR E-BEÏDA

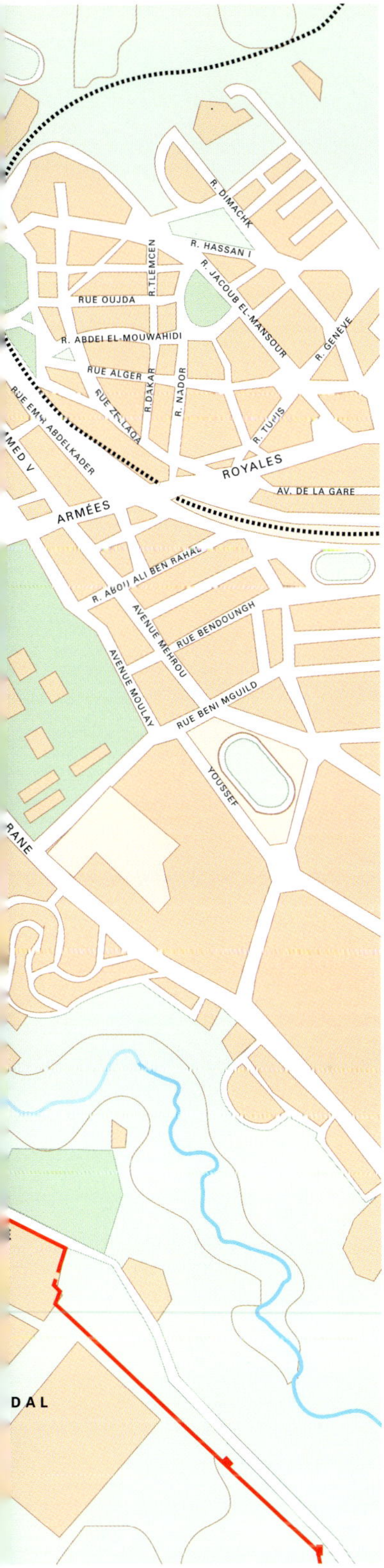

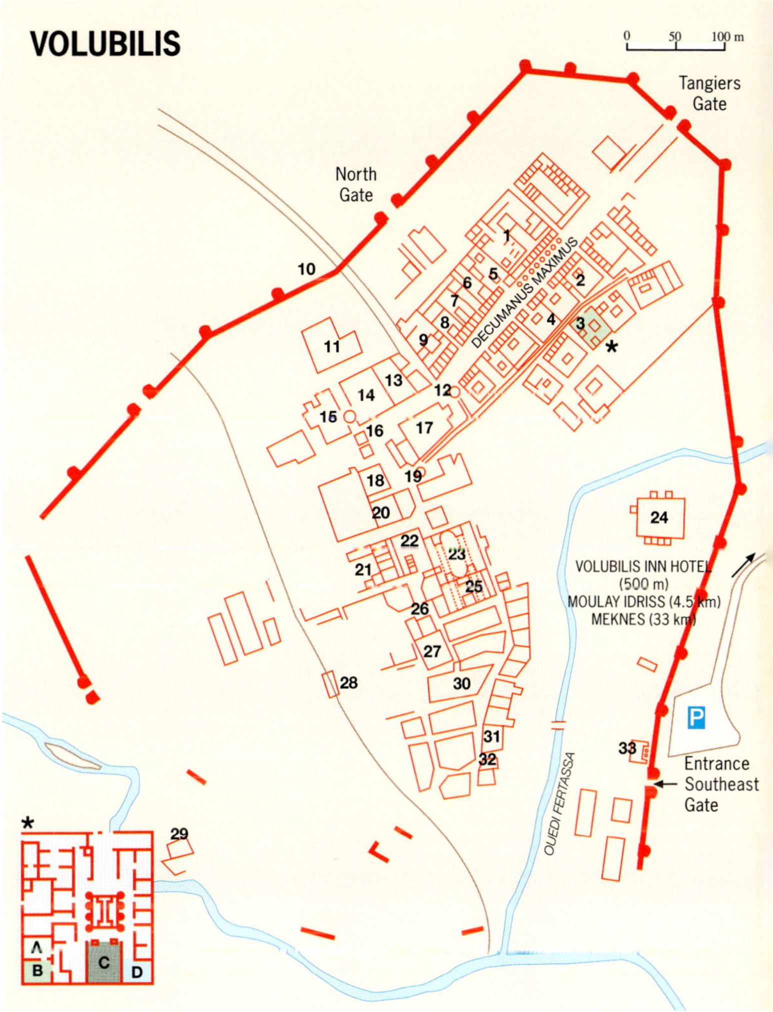

VOLUBILIS

1. The Palace of Gordian
2. House of Bacchus
3. House of Venus
4. House of the Nereids
5. House of the wild animal mosaic
6. House of the Bath of the Nymph
7. House of Dionysus and the Four Seasons
8. House of Flavius Germanus
9. House of the Labours of Hercules
10. Wall of Marcus Aurelius
11. House of the Cistern
12. Fountain
13. House of the Cavalier
14. House of the Columns
15. House of Ephebus
16. Triumphal Arch
17. North baths
18. House of the Dog
19. Fountain
20. House of the Acrobat
21. Bakery
22. Forum
23. Basilica
24. Temple of Saturn
25. Capitol
26. Restored mill
27. Baths of Gallienus
28. Twin temples
29. Baths outside the walls
30. House of Orpheus
31. Skeleton of a woman
32. Oil press
33. Cafeteria

A. Abduction of Hylas by Nymphs
B. Diana Surprised in Her Bath
C. Triclinium
D. Bacchus and the Four Seasons

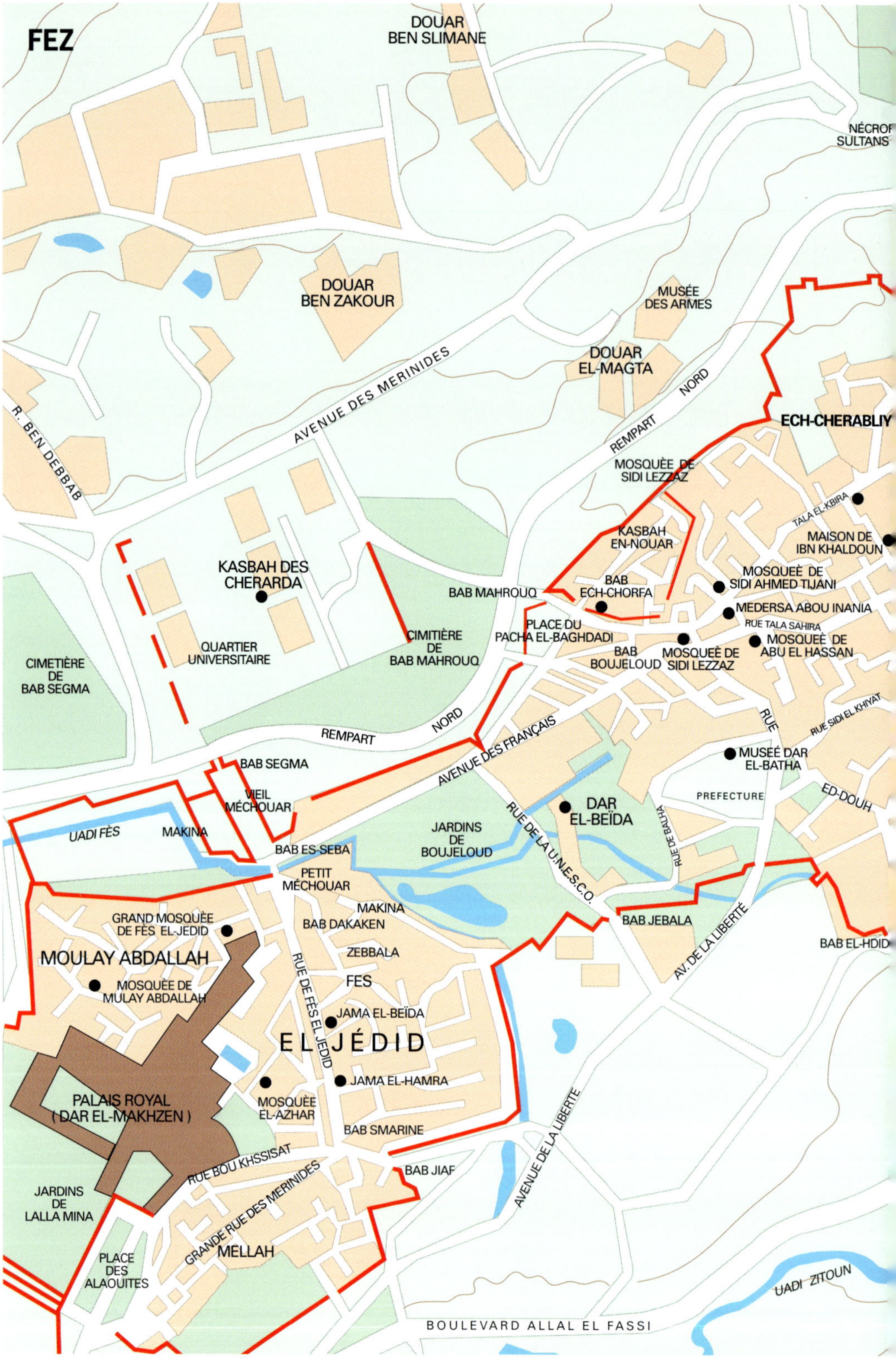
FEZ
DOUAR BEN SLIMANE
NÉCROP SULTANS
DOUAR BEN ZAKOUR
MUSÉE DES ARMES
DOUAR EL-MAGTA
AVENUE DES MERINIDES
R. BEN DEBBAB
REMPART NORD
ECH-CHERABLIY
MOSQUÈE DE SIDI LEZZAZ
TALA EL-KBIRA
MAISON DE IBN KHALDOUN
KASBAH EN-NOUAR
KASBAH DES CHERARDA
BAB MAHROUQ
BAB ECH-CHORFA
MOSQUEÈ DE SIDI AHMED TIJANI
MEDERSA ABOU INANIA
RUE TALA SAHIRA
MOSQUEÈ DE ABU EL HASSAN
PLACE DU PACHA EL-BAGHDADI
CIMITIÈRE DE BAB MAHROUQ
QUARTIER UNIVERSITAIRE
CIMETIÈRE DE BAB SEGMA
BAB BOUJELOUD
MOSQUEÈ DE SIDI LEZZAZ
RUE SIDI EL KHIYAT
RUE ED-DOUH
REMPART NORD
AVENUE DES FRANÇAIS
MUSEÉ DAR EL-BATHA
PREFECTURE
BAB SEGMA
VIEIL MÉCHOUAR
DAR EL-BEÏDA
UADI FÈS
MAKINA
JARDINS DE BOUJELOUD
RUE DE LA U.N.E.S.C.O.
RUE DE BALTHA
BAB ES-SEBA
PETIT MÉCHOUAR
MAKINA
BAB DAKAKEN
GRAND MOSQUÈE DE FÈS EL-JEDID
BAB JEBALA
AV. DE LA LIBERTÉ
BAB EL-HDID
ZEBBALA
MOULAY ABDALLAH
FES
MOSQUÈE DE MULAY ABDALLAH
RUE DE FÈS EL JEDID
JAMA EL-BEÏDA
EL JÉDID
PALAIS ROYAL (DAR EL-MAKHZEN)
JAMA EL-HAMRA
MOSQUÈE EL-AZHAR
BAB SMARINE
AVENUE DE LA LIBERTE
RUE BOU KHSSISAT
BAB JIAF
JARDINS DE LALLA MINA
GRANDE RUE DES MERINIDES
MELLAH
PLACE DES ALAOUITES
UADI ZITOUN
BOULEVARD ALLAL EL FASSI

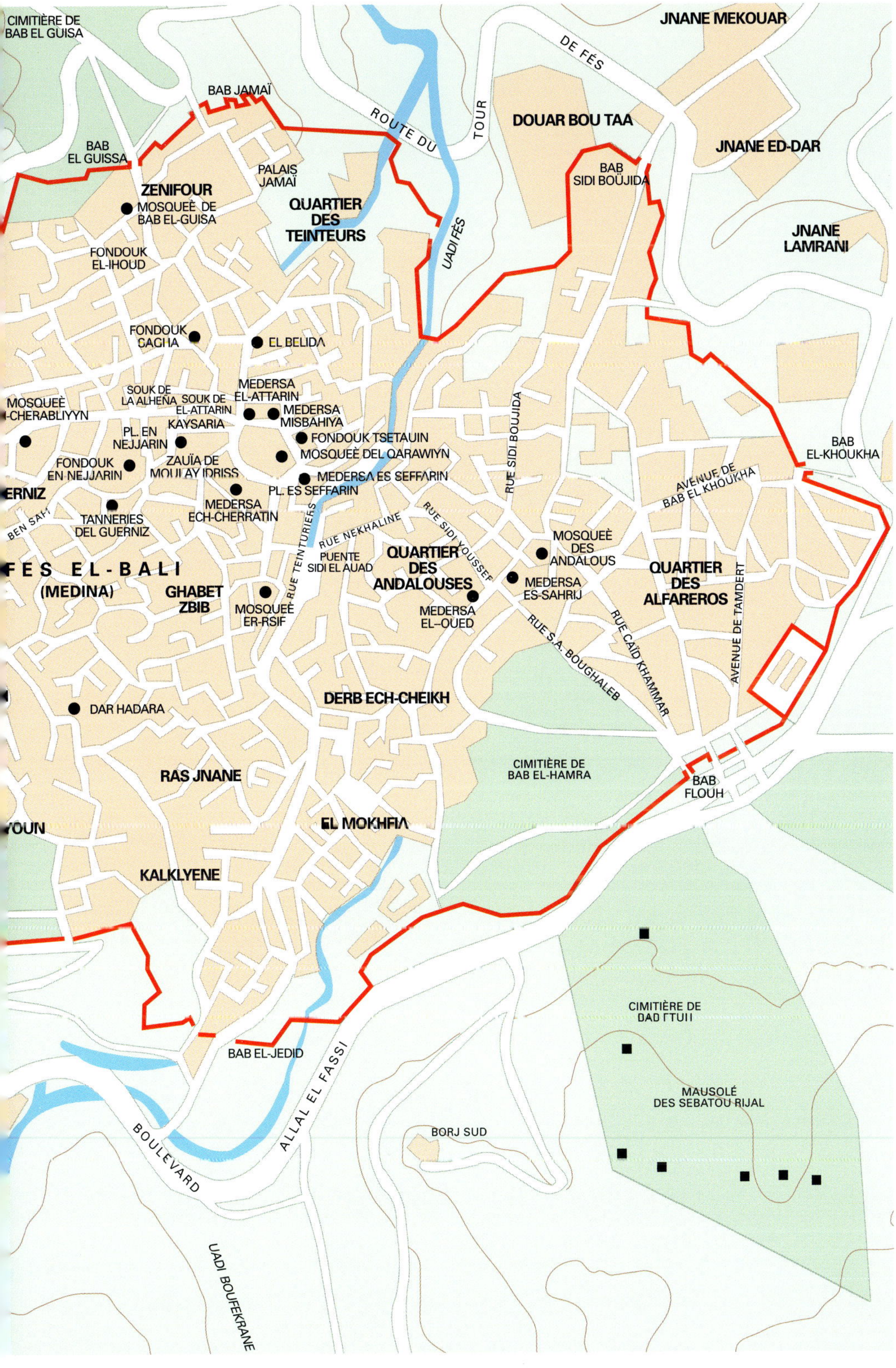
CIMITIÈRE DE BAB EL GUISA
JNANE MEKOUAR
DE FÈS
ROUTE DU
TOUR
BAB JAMAÏ
DOUAR BOU TAA
JNANE ED-DAR
BAB EL GUISSA
PALAIS JAMAÏ
BAB SIDI BOÜJIDA
ZENIFOUR
QUARTIER DES TEINTEURS
MOSQUEÈ DE BAB EL-GUISA
UADI FÈS
JNANE LAMRANI
FONDOUK EL-IHOUD
FONDOUK SAGHA
EL BELIDA
MEDERSA EL-ATTARIN
SOUK DE LA ALHEÑA
SOUK DE EL-ATTARIN
MOSQUEÈ
-CHERABLIYYN
MEDERSA MISBAHIYA
KAYSARIA
RUE SIDI BOUJIDA
PL. EN NEJJARIN
FONDOUK TSETAUIN
MOSQUEÈ DEL QARAWIYN
BAB EL-KHOUKHA
FONDOUK EN NEJJARIN
ZAUÏA DE MOULAY IDRISS
MEDERSA ES SEFFARIN
AVENUE DE BAB EL KHOUKHA
ERNIZ
PL. ES SEFFARIN
MEDERSA ECH-CHERRATIN
BEN SAH
TANNERIES DEL GUERNIZ
RUE NEKHALINE
RUE SIDI YOUSSEF
MOSQUEÈ DES ANDALOUS
FES EL-BALI (MEDINA)
PUENTE SIDI EL AUAD
QUARTIER DES ANDALOUSES
QUARTIER DES ALFAREROS
GHABET ZBIB
RUE TEINTURIERS
MEDERSA ES-SAHRIJ
AVENUE DE TAMDERT
MOSQUEÈ ER-RSIF
MEDERSA EL–OUED
RUE S.A. BOUGHALEB
RUE CAÏD KHAMMAR
DERB ECH-CHEIKH
DAR HADARA
CIMITIÈRE DE BAB EL-HAMRA
BAB FLOUH
RAS JNANE
EL MOKHFIA
YOUN
KALKLYENE
CIMITIÈRE DE
BAB EL-JEDID
MAUSOLÉ DES SEBATOU RIJAL
ALLAL EL FASSI
BORJ SUD
BOULEVARD
UADI BOUFEKRANE

Vers Chez Ali Bel Fallah
15 Marjane
VERS CASABLANCA
VERS EL JADIDA SAFI
Ecôle des Mines
10 Hôpital Ibn Tofaïl
Jardin Majorelle A
Palm Club
D'AOUDIATE
Wilaya de Marrakech
Gare Routière 18
PLACE EL-MOURABITENNE
Bab Doukkala 17
12 GUELIZ
1 Office du Tourisme
Marché Central
Acima Super-marché
PLACE ABD EL MOUMEN BEN ALI
P.T.T. Gueliz 2
PLACE DU 16 NOVEMBRE
Gare Chemin de Fer 3
PLACE DU EMPEREUR HAILE SÉLASSIE
21 Jardin du Hartsi
Commissariat Police
Théâtre Royale
CITÉ NOUVELLE (GUELIZ)
PARC DES SPORTS
PL. DE LA LIBERTÉ
Tribunal
Cadastre
Auberge de Jeunesse 4
5 Camping Caravaning Municipal
Municipalité
Palais de Congrés
Casino
HIVERNAGE
6 Camping Touring Club
BASE MILITAIRE AERIENNE
Jardin de la Ménara
Parc de la Ménara O
VERS ASNI
VERS VALLEE D'OURIKA
VERS L'AEROPORT
VERS TAROUDANT AMIZMIZ
Club Equestre 11
VERS ESSAOUIRA AGADIR
VERS MARJANE EL MASSIRA
Mosquée de Bab Doukkala
Dar el-Glaoui
Hôtel de ville 7
Ensemble artisanal 8
Bab Nkob
ARSET MOULAY ABDESLAM
SQUARE ABD EL-MOUMEN
J Mosquée de la Koutoubia
Consulat de France 19
PL. YOUSSEF BEN TACHFINE
Tombeau Youssef Ben Tachfine
Bab ech-Charia
Bab Aguenaou
Bab er-Rob
Mausolée de Sidi es-Souheyli
Cimetière de Sidi es-Souheyli
Bab el-Jédid
Bab el-Makhzen
Bab er-Raha
Mosquée et de Sidi be
Zauïa de Sid Ibn Sliman el-Ja
Mosquée de Mulay el-Ks
AVENUE MOHAMMED V
BD. MOULAY RACHID
AVENUE HASSAN II
AV. DES NATIONS UNIES
ROUTE DES REMPARTS
AV. HOUMMAN EL-FETOUAKI
AVENUE EL MENARA

Public and administrative buildings in Marrakesh:

1. Tourist Office (Tel: 024 43 61 31)
2. P.T.T. (Post Office) Gueliz
3. Railway Station
4. Youth Hostel
5. Municipal Camping and Caravanning site
6. Touring Club Camping site
7. Town Hall
8. Craft Centre
9. P.T.T. (Post Office) Medina
10. Ibn Tofaïl Hospital
11. Jockey Club
12. Gueliz
13. Royal Palace
14. Mellah
15. Towards Ali Bel Fallah
16. El Mouassine fountain
17. Bab Doukkala
18. Bus station
19. French Consulate
20. Kasbah
21. Jnan du Hartsi
22. Zauïa Sidi Yusuf Ibn Ali
23. Bab el-Khémis

A. Majorelle Garden
B. To the Palmeraie district
C. Almoravid Koubba
D. Madrasa ibn Youssef
E. Tanners district
F. Medina
G. City walls
H. Club Méditerranée
I. Dar-Si-Said Museum of Moroccan Art
J. Koutoubia Mosque
K. Bahia Palace
L. El Badii Palace
M. Bab Agnaou Gate
N. Saadian Tombs
O. Menara Gardens
P. Aguedal Gardens

Place des Artistes
AV MOULAY YOUSSEF
Borj Mellah
Bab Doukala
BORJ. MY. M'HAMED
Rue Zouinate
Rue Chbanate
Rue Chbanate
PLACE BAB MARRAKECH
Rue Zair
Rue Melouyah
Mosquée Abdellah ou Omar
Daoued Ben Aicha
Rue Chaouia
Rue my Smail
Rue Ali Ben Abi Taleb
Rue Al Mourabitine
Rue Ibn Batouta
AV. ZERKTOUNI
Rue Bagdad
Rue Iben Khaldoune
Rue Laghrissi
Rue Zalaqa
Rue Zalaqa
Rue My. Abdelmalek
Palais Heure Bleue
BAB MARRAKECH
Rue Doukkala
Yamouk
Rue Malah
Derb Rqiq
Rue Tafilalte
Rue Ellabbana
Rue My. Ismail
Rue Bouchantouf
Rue El Hourya
Complex Artisanal
Delg. d'Artisanat
Rue El Kousse
Rue Tunis
Rue Boutouile
Bani Marrine
Sidi Kasem
Mosquée AL Baouakhir
Brahim Addounia
Rue Sidi Ali Abdellah
BORJ BAB MARRAKECH La Citadelle Mohamedia
Rue Salé
Marché de volailles
Rue Ben Laghazi
Rue Ibn Khaldoune
AV MOHAMED EL QORI
Mosquée Haha
Rue de Misr
Rue Agadir
Ouazzan
Rue Qaraouyine
Ruew Boutouile
Rue Annaser
Rue Ben Laghazi
Rue Sayaghine
Rue Sidi Laghazy
Place marché de grains
RUE SOUK JDID
Rue Algerie
Rue Kasem El Abbare
My. Abderahman
Mosquée Jbala
Rue Jbala
Marché de poissons ey épices
La Joutia
Mosquée Haha
Rue Kowait
Rue Menjra
Rue Sayaghine
Rue El Khabbazine
Derb Ali El Moudden
Si Allal El Ouaqaoui
My. Azouze
Mosquée Ahmad ou Med
Bijoutiers
Rue El Haouz
Mosquée Ahl Agadir
Chefchaouen
Rue My. Slimane
Rue Abdelaziz El Fechtaly
Rue Tanger
Tripoli
Rue Abou Al Mahajire
Rue Kowait
Rue Biroute
Rue Oujda
AV. L'ISTIQLAL
Rue Qadi Ayad
Rue Khader Ghallan
Rue Al Mouahidin
Rue Youssef Ben Tachfine
Rue Malek Ben Morahhal
Rue Agadir
Rue D'oum Rabia
Oura
Mosquée Amsguina
Rue Sidi Ahmed Haroun
Rue Touahen
Rue Ceuta
AV. SIDI MOHAMED BEN ABDELLAH
Rue Qadisiya
Rue Sidi Abdesmih
Bab Al Bahar
Rue Touahen
Rue Abderahmane Eddakhil
Rue Ahmed Baba Soudany
Mosquée Ben Youssef
Rue Ceuta
Mosquée Dar Dheb
Rue Abdessalam Labbadi
Mosquée Al Attarine
Administration des Habousses
Rue Dar Dheb
Rue Mokite
Riad Dar El Pacha
Rue Daraa
Espace Otello
Layachi
Bab Sbâa
Mosquée Oueld Bihi
Rue Zayan
Riad Al Madina
Rue de Rif
Rue Lattarine
Rue Mohamed
Abbas Essaadi
Galerie Bab Sbaa
Dar Souri
Centre de Santé
Saadiene
Rue Sidi Ali Ben Daoud
Rue Zayan
Dar Music
Rue de Marrakech
Ancien Consulat Danois
Commissariat de Police
Office du Torisme
Rue Mohamed Ben Masoud
Mosquée Sid Ali Ben Daoud
Galertie Orange Bleu
Place Chirb Atai
Av. Allal Ben Abdellah
Houmman Fatouaki
L'Horloge
Rue Youssef El Fassy
Rue Yamen
Rue Touahen
Surya
Sidi Magdoul
Rue Ziry Ben Atiyah
Rue Tetouan
Place Chefchaouni
AV. Oqba Ibn Nafiaa
Bab Ljhad
Rue Yamen
Darb Lalouj
Musée Sidi Med. Ben Abdellah
Rue Iben Toumarte
Rue My. Rachid
Rue El Hajjali
Rue Abdellah Ben Yassin
Ancien Consulat de France
Rue Mohamed Diouri
Ancien Consulat d'Italie
Mosquée La Kasbah
Bab Dar El Maghzen
Place Orson Welles
Rue Ibn Rochd
Salle Couverte
Rue Moussa Ben Noussair
Porte de Chayla
Skala de la Kasbah
Ancienne Eglise Portuguaise
Rue Ibn Zohr
Rue Khaled Ben Oualid
Bab Kasar
Ancienne Palais de Justice
Place MOULAY HASSAN
Bab El Menzah
Rue Sakala
Rue du Souss
Bab Laachour
PARKING
Bhar Club
Bastion Ouest
Grillades Sardines
Délégation Maritime
Arrondi du Port
O.N.P
Océan Atlantique
Douanes
Halle Aux Poisons
O.D.E.P
Porte Maritime
Skala du Port
ESSAOUIRA

AGADIR
Océan Atlantique
Avenue Al Moun
Hôspital Hassan II
Lotissement Taddart
Village de L'Electricien
Cimtières
Lycée
Lotissement Charaf
Mohammed Cheikh Saadi
L'Aéroport Almassira
Les Amicales
Anquar Souss
Quartier Résidentiel
Avenue al Moun
Polyclinique
Avenue Moulay Youssef
Lotissement Marins Pêcheurs
Lotissement An-Najah
Rue Abdellah Ben Yassine
La Marina
Port de pêche
Port de plaisance
Boulevard Mohammed V
CAMPING
Avenue Général el Kettani
Jardin Olhao
Mosquée Loubnane
Rue Mansour
Avenue Moulay Ismail
Stade Najh Souss
Avenue Imam Al Boukhari
Mosquée Mohammed V
Talborjt
Avenue Tawada
Piscine d'Agadir
Vallée des Oiseaux
Place Alamal
Hôtel de ville
Rue du 29 Février
Rue Ibn Batouta
Rue du 18 Novembre
Ma Lainine
Jardin Prince Heritier
Rue President Kennedy
Quartier Industriel
Rue du 9 Juillet
Secteur Touristique
Avenue du Prince Moulay Abdallah
Hassan II
Rue Moussa ibn Noussair
Rue Quadi Ayyad
Quartier Industriel
Musée Municipal
Stade Alinbiat
Stade Alinbiat Sud
Avenue al Mouqaouama
Jardin Lala Mariam
Rue du 2 Mars
Rue Omar Al Khayam
Boulevard du 20 Août
Rue Oued Souss
Stade Abdellah Didi
Souk al Had
Rue chair Alhambra
Avenue el Hassan II
Rue Wadnfis
Secteur Touristique
Palais Royal
Mohammed Ben Brahim

TANGIER
PORT DE TANGER
BAIE DE TANGER
QCAR MARCHAN
AVENUE DES U.S.A.
STADE MUNICIPAL
DRADEB
AVENUE AL IMAM MALIK
AVENUE HASSAN II
ANCIENNE MEDINA
LA MONTAGNE
PALAIS ITALIEN
IBN HAZM
AVENUE HASSAN I
DOUANES
GRAND MOSQUÉE
PLACE 9 AVRIL 1947
PORTUGAL
TARIK AYN AL HAYYANI
SIDI BOU'DIB
WALILI AD DIN AL AYYOUBI
AVENUE D'ESPAGNE
GARE
AL IMAM AL QOST ALANI
CASABLANCA
IBN ZAYDOUN
AVENUE SIDI MOHAMED BEN ABDALLAH
BELGIQUE
MOSQUÉE
SAHET FRANCE
INSTITUT ESPAGNOL
MEXIQUE
LAMÇALLA
AVENUE DES F.A.R.
HÔPITAL DUC DE TOVAR
HÔPITAL ESPAGNOL
MOUSSA IBN NOÇAYI
AVENUE MOHAMED V
ANTAKI
HÔPITAL HAMED V
SAHET WAD AL MAKHAZIN
AVENUE ALLAL BEN ABDALLAH
AV. AL MOUKAWAMA
SAHET AL OUMAM
AVENUE YOUSSEF IBN TACHAFINE
CENTRE CULTUREL FRANÇAIS
SAHET BRAHIM AR-ROUDANI
AVENUE HARCUM
AV. ANGLATERRE
IBN TOFAYL
AL JAZIRA
SAHET AL MADINA
AVENUE IBN AL HAYLEM
AVENUE WAJDA
EGLISE FRANÇAISE
AVENUE AL IMAM BEN TAYMIYA
AVENUE BEETHOVEN
GIBRALTAR
ANDALOUSSI
PRINCE HERITIER
AV. OMAR IBN AL KHATTAB
IBN JAROUM
AVENUE ABI JARIR AL TABARI
GARE ROUTIÈRE
HAY LALLA CHAFYA
AVENUE HASSAN AD-DAKHIL
SAHET BIR ANZARANE
AV. MOULAY YOUSSEF
SAHET ABDAL'AZIZ
AVENUE IDRISSI
ACH CHIKH MIYYARA
WAD ZIZ
PLACE 20 AOÛT
AL QADI 'AWAD
AVENUE HASSAN ACH CHADLI
SAHET AL JAMI'A AL ARABIYA
AVENUE HAROUN AR-RA

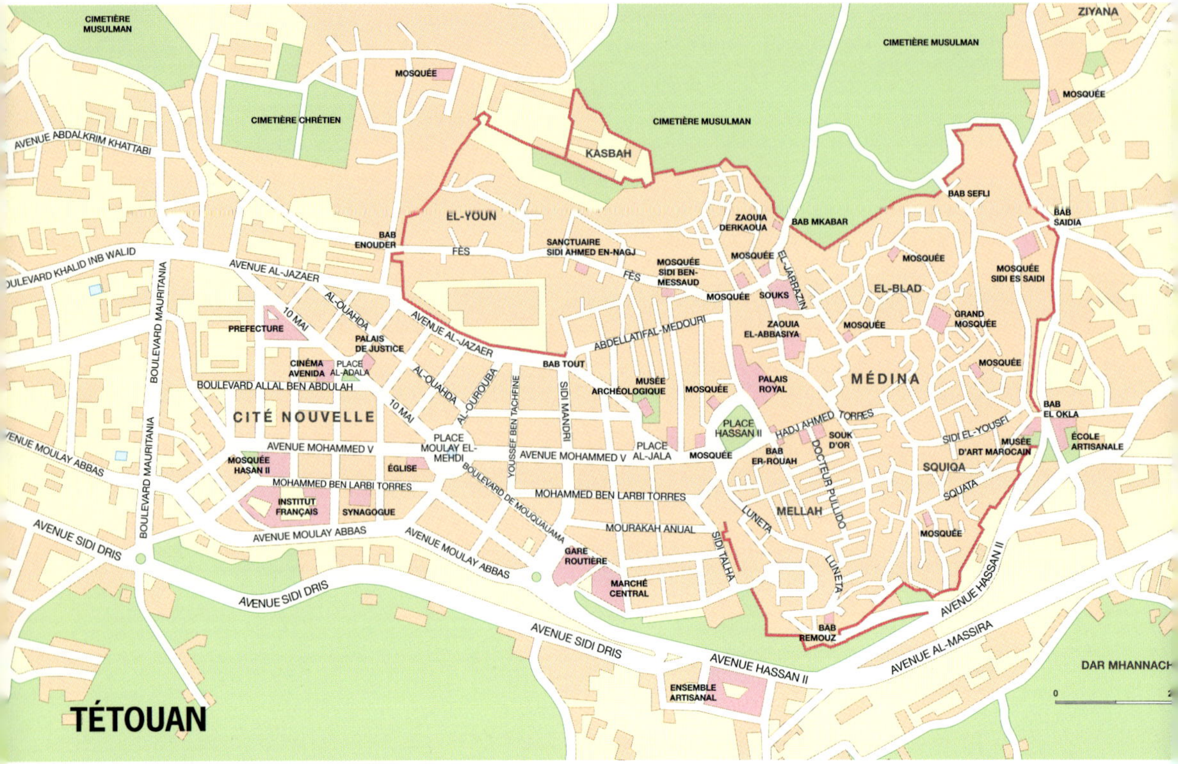
TÉTOUAN
CIMETIÈRE MUSULMAN
MOSQUÉE
CIMETIÈRE CHRÉTIEN
CIMETIÈRE MUSULMAN
ZIYANA
AVENUE ABDALKRIM KHATTABI
KASBAH
EL-YOUN
BAB ENOUDER
FÈS
SANCTUAIRE SIDI AHMED EN-NAGJ
ZAOUIA DERKAOUA
BAB MKABAR
BAB SEFLI
BAB SAIDIA
BOULEVARD KHALID INB WALID
AVENUE AL-JAZAER
MOSQUÉE SIDI BEN-MESSAOUD
MOSQUÉE
SOUKS
EL-JARRAZIN
EL-BLAD
MOSQUÉE SIDI ES SAIDI
GRAND MOSQUÉE
BOULEVARD MAURITANIA
PREFECTURE
10 MAI
AL-OUAHDA
PALAIS DE JUSTICE
AVENUE AL-JAZAER
ABDELLATIFAL-MEDOURI
ZAOUIA EL-ABBASIYA
BAB TOUT
CINÉMA AVENIDA
PLACE AL-ADALA
BOULEVARD ALLAL BEN ABDULAH
MUSÉE ARCHÉOLOGIQUE
PALAIS ROYAL
MÉDINA
BAB EL OKLA
CITÉ NOUVELLE
10 MAI
AL-OUROUBA
YOUSSEF BEN TACHFINE
SIDI MANDRI
PLACE HASSAN II
HADJ AHMED TORRES
SOUK D'OR
SIDI EL-YOUSFI
MUSÉE D'ART MAROCAIN
ÉCOLE ARTISANALE
AVENUE MOULAY ABBAS
AVENUE MOHAMMED V
PLACE MOULAY EL-MEHDI
AVENUE MOHAMMED V
PLACE AL-JALA
BAB ER-ROUAH
SQUIQA
MOSQUÉE HASAN II
ÉGLISE
MOHAMMED BEN LARBI TORRES
INSTITUT FRANÇAIS
SYNAGOGUE
BOULEVARD DE MOUQUAUAMA
MOHAMMED BEN LARBI TORRES
DOCTEUR PULIDO
SQUATA
MELLAH
LUNETA
AVENUE SIDI DRIS
AVENUE MOULAY ABBAS
AVENUE MOULAY ABBAS
MOURAKAH ANUAL
SIDI TALHA
GARE ROUTIÈRE
MARCHÉ CENTRAL
AVENUE HASSAN II
AVENUE SIDI DRIS
BAB REMOUZ
AVENUE SIDI DRIS
AVENUE HASSAN II
AVENUE AL-MASSIRA
DAR MHANNACH
ENSEMBLE ARTISANAL
0

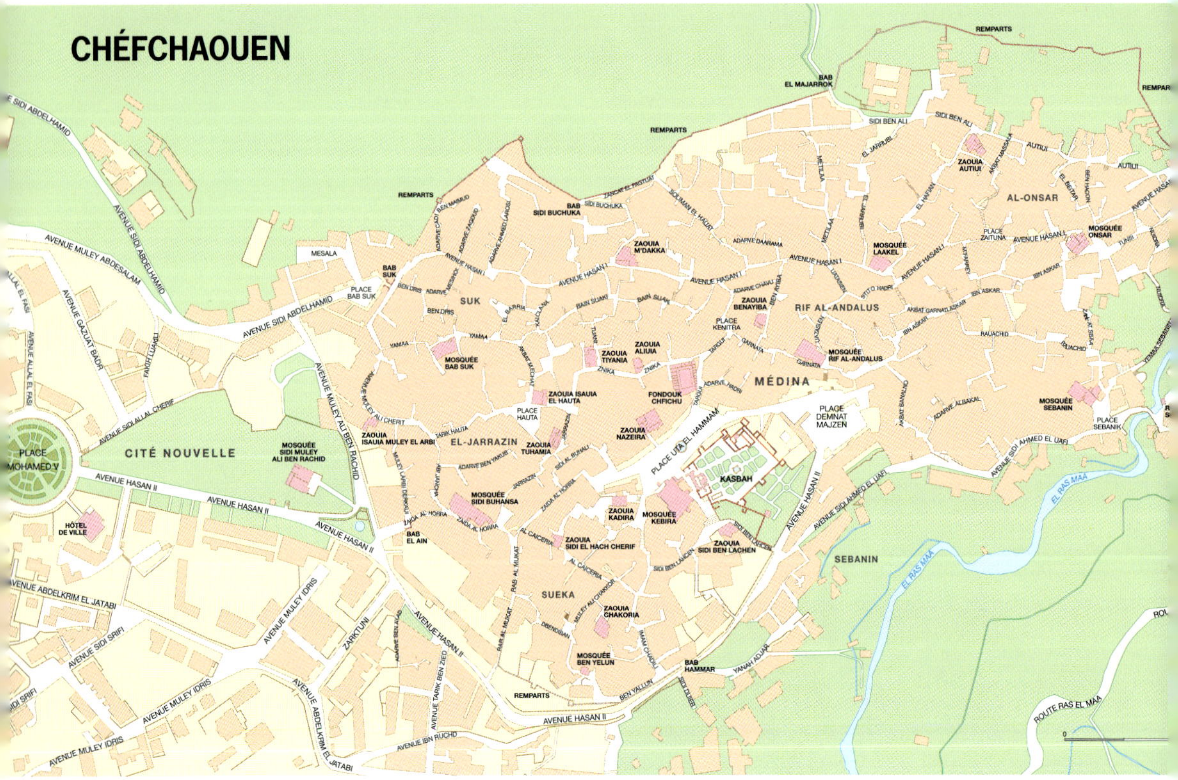
CHÉFCHAOUEN
REMPARTS
BAB EL MAJARROK
REMPARTS
AVENUE SIDI ABDELHAMID
REMPARTS
BAB SIDI BUCHUKA
ZAOUIA AUTIUI
AL-ONSAR
AVENUE MULEY ABDESALAM
MESALA
BAB SUK
PLACE BAB SUK
ZAOUIA M'DAKKA
MOSQUÉE LAAKEL
MOSQUÉE ONSAR
AVENUE SIDI ABDELHAMID
SUK
ZAOUIA BENAYIBA
PLACE KENITRA
RIF AL-ANDALUS
ZAOUIA TIYANIA
ZAOUIA ALIUIA
MOSQUÉE RIF AL-ANDALUS
MOSQUÉE BAB SUK
FONDOUK CHFICHU
MÉDINA
ZAOUIA ISAUIA EL HAUTA
MOSQUÉE SEBANIN
PLACE SEBANIK
PLACE HAUTA
PLACE DEMNAT MAJZEN
ZAOUIA ISAUIA MULEY EL ARBI
EL-JARRAZIN
ZAOUIA TUHAMIA
ZAOUIA NAZEIRA
PLACE UTA EL HAMMAM
AVENUE SIDI AHMED EL UAFI
PLACE MOHAMED V
CITÉ NOUVELLE
MOSQUÉE SIDI MULEY ALI BEN RACHID
AVENUE MULEY ALI BEN RACHID
KASBAH
AVENUE HASAN II
AVENUE HASAN II
MOSQUÉE SIDI BUHANSA
ZAOUIA KADIRA
MOSQUÉE KEBIRA
HÔTEL DE VILLE
AVENUE HASAN II
BAB EL AIN
ZAOUIA SIDI EL HACH CHERIF
ZAOUIA SIDI BEN LACHEN
SEBANIN
EL RAS MAA
AVENUE ABDELKRIM EL JATABI
SUEKA
ZAOUIA CHAKORIA
AVENUE MULEY IDRIS
AVENUE SIDI SRIFI
MOSQUÉE BEN YELUN
BAB HAMMAR
AVENUE HASAN II
REMPARTS
AVENUE HASAN II
AVENUE MULEY IDRIS
AVENUE ABDELKRIM EL JATABI
AVENUE IBN RUCHD
AVENUE MULEY IDRIS
ROUTE RAS EL MAA
0

المملكة المغربية
MOROCCO
SCALE
50 0 50 100 150 200 250 Km.
LEGEND
MAIN ROAD
SECONDARY ROAD
RAILROAD LINE
BOUNDARY
PORTUGAL
CORDOBA
JAEN
HUELVA
SEVILLA
ESPAGNE
GRANADA
ALMERIA
MALAGA
CADIZ
ALGECIRAS
GIBRALTAR
MER MEDITERRANEE
TANGER
SEBTA
CAP ESPARTEL
TETOUAN
ASILAH
MELILLA
CHECHAOUEN
AL HOCEIMA
GHAZAOUET
LARACHE
NADOR
BERKANE
OUEZZANE
TARGUISTE
OUJDA
TAOUNATE
TAOURIRT
KENITRA
SIDI KACEM
RABAT
FES
TAZA
GUERCIF
AIN BENI MATHAR
SEFROU
MEKNES
KHEMISSET
CASABLANCA
BEN SLIMANE
ATLAS
BOULMANE
BERRECHID
AZROU
EL JADIDA
SETTAT
KHOURIBGA
KHENIFRA
BOUÂRFA
MIDELT
BENI MELLAL
SAFI
YOUSSOUFIA
EL KELAA DES
SRARHNA
AZILAL
MOYEN
RACHIDIA
BOUDNIB
GOULMINA
MARRAKECH
DEMNATE
BECHAR
ESSAOUIRA
ERFOUD
TINERHIR
ABADLA
HAUT
OUARZAZATE
RISSANI
TAMANAR
MERZOUGA
TAROUDANNT
AGADIR
TALIOUINE
ZAGORA
BENI ABBÉS
TAFRAOUTE
TABELBALA
TIZNIT
ANTI
SIDI IFNI
GOULIMINE
TINFOUCHY
ATLANTIQUE
LES ILES CANARIES
Lanzarote
Tenerife
Fuerteventura
Gomera
Gran Canaria
TAN-TAN
ZAG
TARFAYA
TINDOUF
AL HAGGOUNIYA
DAWRA
AL MAHBAS
JDIRIYA
FARCIYA
LA YOUN
HAWZA
AD-DCHIRA
BOU BURNOUS
GARAT JBILET
SEMARA
BOUKRAA
AMGALA
BIR LAHLOU
OCEAN
BOUJDOUR
TFARITY
AIN BE TILI
GUELTAT ZEMMOUR
CHEGGA
ERG CHECH
OUM DRAYGA
BIR ANZARAN
AD-DAKHALA
MAURITANIE
AWSARD
AZ-ZOUIRAT
MALI
AGNAYLAS
BIR GANDOUZ
TECHLA
ZOUG

CONTENTS

Fotolia.com: #2610009 © jakezc – #9242840 © Pictures news – #11474996, #52815252 © philipus – #11918658 © irabel8 – #23937996 © Stefanie Haubert – #35755533 © luisapuccini – #38913135 © Anibal Trejo – #42272814, #42272826 © kicimici – #53040411 © Xavier Allard – #58124611 © pulpitis17 – #63411758, #70999813, #70999954 © evannovostro – #71940649 © megastocker – #73245839 © amskad – #83293140 © françoise bro – #85385959, #89795085, #232081775 © Noradoa – #88813735 © Ariane Citron – #91763220 © cornfield – #99139572 © Álvaro Germán Vilela – #103919302 © Rechitan Sorin – #105107980, #115002163 © javarman – #106345326 © vladislav333222 – #113421327 © jefwod – #122030465, #122031070, #122031610, #122031676, #122031743, #122031814, #122032360, #170334734, #170334854, #170335022, #170335032, #186040375, #186040878, #186040950, #199815291, #200629150, #200629204, #200629219, #225485185, #225485543, #225485569 © saiko3p – #122094659 © Crin – #124165281 © Marc Jedamus – #125925621, #126318604 © majonit – #130404406, #130407306 © Rechitan Sorin – #131998972 © Laurens – #132881066 © Frozen Action – #133695252 © rudiernst – #135099299, #135099375, #135986428, #140716992 © Jose Ignacio Soto – #137886751, #176384819, #177077573 © Elena Odareeva – #139249212, #139469838, #139731437, #139806799, #140255309, #141051602, #141513096, #141624931, #141625202 © Leonid Andronov – #139631379 © Julian Schaldach – #145418427 © ynos – #145432662, #147473028, #155743565, #155743627, #155743639 © milosk50 – #150691006 © mrcatmint – #161171277 © Carlos Neto – #162554194 © evenfh – #162888842 © jon_chica – #166186960 © fotosaga – #167149805 © tinasdreamworld – #168016683 © kasto – #168806108, #168815743 © siempreverde22 – #172678290 © Fabian – #173666934 © fotosaga – #174760880 © louis – #176714608 © Vlada Z – #178842635 © Jan – #180210007 © Francesco Bonino – #182518925 © jon_chica – #187194380 © dinozzaver – #192990354 © Monique Pouzet – #195724461 © Andrey Shevchenko – #197400454 © banepetkovic – #198180782 © Anneke – #198308531 © ivanovevgeniy – #201622901 © xabi – #204654887 © Saharrr – #205255781, #205257326 © Pierre-Yves Babelon – #207204215 © kino1493 – #209739732 © Can – #209983680 © Balate Dorin – #211086347 © Egon Boemsch – #213393528, #232547479 © Kotangens – #213982435 © Robson90 – #216427515 © Antoine – #216980635, #216980653 © Loui Photo – #220550256 © Louis-Michel DESERT – #224838004 © Cezary Wojtkowski – #228874617 © juanorihuela – #230139798 © olenatur – #230277502 © pszabo – #232794280, #233168450, #233205360 © Vixit – #233009690 © Jan Marot – #233081139 © Don Whitebread – #236246628, #242083587, #251003788 © mitzo_bs – #236846025, #249216099 © Olena Z – #237811214 © KajzrPhotography.com – #237935037 © dsaprin – #238158642, #243704546 © sark181095 – #241864454 © imadtouil – #242390050 © Adi Seres – #242669866 © Tarik GOK – #244535321, #244535373, #244535824 © Craig – #245385062, #245385119 © Valery Bareta.

EDITORIAL FISA ESCUDO DE ORO, S.A.
Tel: +34 93 230 86 00
www.eoro.com

I.S.B.N. 978-84-378-3284-5
Printed in Spain
Legal Dep. B. 10082-2019